I have a question for the 35 million-plus parents and related caregivers of special-needs children of **any** diagnosis, cognitive or physical, which, according to various research, live in the United States: Have you ever been at the wall? At the end of your rope? Slammed? Fed up? Call it whatever you want, the emotions are the same: numb from overwhelming news about your child or children, making you feel as if you're in a box, not knowing how to get out, or even having the desire or the energy to deal with whatever *the news* is.

Most would say yes, they've been there, regardless of who they are. Everyone's been at the wall at times. So when it happens, how do *you* deal with it? And how does it impact your personal life, work life, marriage, relationships, family and beliefs? Is there a process you follow when tragic or unexpected things happen to help you move forward with a renewed outlook and sense of purpose? This book will give you one, one that will serve and endure. A process developed over years of caring for my son with special needs, and from being so slammed that all I could do was look up and yell, *"Enough is enough!"* You know the expression, *"When the going gets tough, the tough get going"*? Well, I couldn't get going. For years, I was paralyzed with emotional trauma, feeling as though I was in a bottomless pit and couldn't get out, regardless of how much I tried. Allow me to explain.

Nobody expects or even thinks about having a child that isn't *perfect* in every way. At least I never did. I'd been blessed with a beautiful, athletic, accomplished, driven daughter of whom I was very proud, and now a son. What will we do together? What sports will he play? How tall will he be? And when he gets married, he too will have a family and I'll be a grandfather.

Images of our future went racing through my mind like candy being offered to a child, as if I could reach out and select just those pieces I wanted for my son. I had it all mapped out as if I were in charge. When *the news* was presented months after his second birthday, everything stopped and shifted into a slow-motion movie. My son was clinically diagnosed with Williams Syndrome, something my family, friends and some doctors had never heard of, or didn't know much about.

Williams is a genetic abnormality in the brain where Connor is minus approximately 20 genes around chromosome seven. This *gene deletion* ends up impacting basical and gross motor skills, cognitive abilities, hi , heart, blood pressure, what he'll eat, his his understanding or appreciation of other people's need for boundaries, and many other things that affect his daily life forever!

For a forward-looking type A, the news put me in a state of numbness. I didn't want to do anything other than learn about Williams, understand the ramifications for Connor, cope with a destroyed *perfect picture* of how life was going to be, and try to fit the pieces together as to what a totally different life looked like going forward. I needed to manage the things that happened to our family, our marriage and our life, while trying to stay positive, hopeful and halfway optimistic. Ever been at war with life? And in the process of all the anguish, and learning to be a full-time mom and dad, I was taught some of the most amazingly simple lessons about life from my cognitively challenged son—a child teaching me **lasting principles** about how to get the most from what's been put in your path and then—*moving forward.* It was as if he were telling me to ***Reach For Me,*** or reach for him, as I wanted the peace he seemed to have inside, as my life swirled with worry about how to care for him, change my life to support what he needed and learn how to become a caregiver. Suddenly, becoming a caregiver, something very foreign to almost everyone, while trying to manage everything else with a "happy face" at the same time, seemed to be my new calling! Something I wasn't expecting.

This is a true story about how I came to learn of my son's syndrome, touching stories about what he has given many, how the stress and strain impacted our family—tragedies and all—and the healing impact he has had on the family and countless others just by being himself. The principles he has taught me, and many others, may end up positively impacting your personal and professional life, and all those with whom you interact. Open your heart, enjoy the story, and allow *The Connor Principles* to touch your life.

Michael A. Boylan is a best-selling author and founder of **The Reach For Me Network**, an Internet-based membership community for parents and related caregivers of special-needs children of **any** diagnosis—cognitive or physical, and the organizations who employ them. The network helps caregivers help one another through the sharing of their stories, knowledge and personal experience, helping them find acknowledgement, emotional support, recognition, encouragement and helpful information, empowering/inspiring them to move forward as best they can as a caregiver of a special-needs child. *Reach For Me* also provides **life-changing** seminars throughout the country for couples, single caregivers, siblings of special-needs children, and families who may be involved in providing care. These programs share a process caregivers can use to **reduce family stress** and **anxiety**, fostering a renewed, more positive outlook and sense of purpose to carry forward throughout their caregiver journey.

The network will expand to include a place caregivers can go on a local level, through a network of Certified Facilitators hosting support group meetings; helping caregivers find respite, community, friendship, recognition and determination to keep moving forward in the care of their special-needs children as they deal with the challenges that have entered their paths.

Reach For Me offers organizations enterprise memberships in the network for employee caregivers (typically 10+ percent of employee population) to join the network and/or attend a seminar, benefiting organizations financially. For information on joining the network or attending a *Caregiver Weekend Summit*, ordering copies of the book for your caregiver friends and family, or inviting the **author to speak** at your organization or church, please visit **www. ReachForMeNetwork.com**. A portion of the proceeds from this book go to The Reach For Me Network to support its mission of providing emotional support, recognition, ongoing encouragement and financial savings for parents of special-needs children of any diagnosis—cognitive or physical. We invite you to **share your feedback** on the book via our website. Thank you, and enjoy the story!

Reach for Me

THE STORY OF MY SON CONNOR

As Dr. Stephen Covey's *Seven Habits* from the international best-selling book and training program *The Seven Habits of Highly Effective People* have positively impacted the lives of millions of people, helping them accomplish more of their dreams, goals and aspirations, *The Connor Principles* are destined to be just as beneficial for the millions of us who are parents and related caregivers of special-needs children throughout the U. S. and around the world.

The Connor Principles are timeless, genuine, forthright principles designed to speak to and address the range of emotional, psychological, physical, spiritual and financial challenges that are a part of any caregiver's life from the moment they first learn of their child's diagnosis. They are designed to help calm and center you, helping you cope, and reduce the stress, anxiety and doubt that often accompanies the role of caregiver. They can help you gain perspective and discover a newfound energy to empower you and your family through the sometimes intensely challenging times, to move forward with a renewed outlook and sense of purpose. Let these timeless principles find their way into your everyday life as you move forward on your journey as a caregiver of a special-needs child.

Be blessed and move forward …

—Michael A. Boylan

Creator, *The Connor Principles Family Home Study Program*

Author, *Reach For Me, The Story of My Son Connor*

Founder, The Reach For Me Network

Reach for Me

THE STORY OF MY SON CONNOR

Life Lessons Learned From My Special-Needs Son Diagnosed With
Williams Syndrome That Will Benefit Your Life And Your Work

BY MICHAEL A. BOYLAN

Reach for Me
The Story of My Son Connor

Published in New York, New York, by Morgan James Publishing. Morgan James and The Entrepreneurial Publisher are trademarks of Morgan James, LLC. www.MorganJamesPublishing.com

The Morgan James Speakers Group can bring authors to your live event. For more information or to book an event visit The Morgan James Speakers Group at www.TheMorganJamesSpeakersGroup.com.

All photographs herein by Michael A. Boylan and Robert M. Boylan. Further, all photographs herein are owned by, and the property of Michael A. Boylan, the copyright owner of this work.

The Connor Principles in whole or in part, The Reach For Me Network, Reach For Me Seminars, Reach For Me, RFM, The RFM Network, The Reach For Me Foundation, Caring For The Caregiver, The Caregiver Weekend Summit, and all related marks are trademarks, registered trademarks and service marks of The Reach For Me Network, LLC. All rights reserved. Reach For Me protects its rights in its marks.

Shelfie

A **free** eBook edition is available
with the purchase of this print book.

CLEARLY PRINT YOUR NAME ABOVE IN UPPER CASE

Instructions to claim your free eBook edition:
1. Download the Shelfie app for Android or iOS
2. Write your name in **UPPER CASE** above
3. Use the Shelfie app to submit a photo
4. Download your eBook to any device

ISBN 978-1-68350-023-0 paperback
ISBN 978-1-68350-024-7 eBook
Library of Congress Control Number:
2016906517

Morgan James
The Entrepreneurial Publisher™

Builds

with...

Habitat for Humanity®
Peninsula and
Greater Williamsburg

In an effort to support local communities, raise awareness and funds, Morgan James Publishing donates a percentage of all book sales for the life of each book to Habitat for Humanity Peninsula and Greater Williamsburg.

Get involved today! Visit
www.MorganJamesBuilds.com

This book is dedicated to my son Connor and my daughter, the apples of my eyes and heart. From them I have learned much about love, suffering, service and gentleness—attributes so important and necessary to raise our children. Likewise, these attributes are desperately needed in the workplace, as all too often, it seems as if it's *all* about the dollar.

I also dedicate this work to the *millions* of parents and families caring for their special-needs children. You are not alone, though you may feel that way, as I do when things get really tough and there doesn't seem to be any end in sight. It is so easy to feel all by yourself when you are the parent of a special-needs child. It's overwhelmingly difficult sometimes, emotionally and psychologically—and lonely.

This book is *not* about finding a cure or focusing awareness on any one particular special need, nor on potential causes or contributors to any one special need. There are several books that focus their energies in this vein, raising the general consciousness, which is absolutely needed. By sharing my story and experience as the single father of a special-needs child—offering it up and putting it out there, my hope is that it will provide encouragement and inspiration for the *millions* of caregivers of special-needs children throughout the world. That's right, *millions*. Some 35 million according to various articles and reports, just in the U.S. alone.

It is not difficult to imagine any parent saying something like, *"In all honesty, my children are most important to me. At the end of the day, that's what it's all about, being there for them, and making sure they have what they need to have a good life."*

There are *few* things more important to parents than the health, happiness, safety, long-term stability and success of their children. Therefore, when parents first learn *the news* that their child has been diagnosed with a *cognitive* and/or a *physical* special need or condition that may well be present for the rest of their child's life, this news often *rocks* their world in several ways—regardless of who they are, how *strong* they are as a person, or how *accomplished* they may be. It challenges the foundations of their own belief system, level of faith, career pursuits, work life, family life, marital or significant relationship, their dreams and goals for the future, and many other areas. It impacts *everything!*

Any parent of a special-needs child will admit that this *news* impacts them emotionally, psychologically, spiritually and financially. Then begins the often *lifelong* process of learning about your child's particular diagnosis to help them as best you can, advocating for them, while learning to deal with and manage all the unknowns ahead; the added pressures/stresses upon other family members, the marriage or significant relationship, the finances, etc., while continuing to carry on with your job and other life commitments.

Hence, it is not a stretch to say that this large group of parents and related caregivers of special-needs children have been handed significant life challenges, which will likely be present until they pass away, then continue on long after they've left this earth. This *truth* creates an opportunity to help this significantly large audience digest, understand, frame, cope with and manage the stresses and challenges over a lifetime, helping them find inspiration, empowerment and strength to continue moving forward as best they can *without* becoming bitter, depressed, angry, negative or withdrawn. Instead, to become *empowered and prepared* for a special life on behalf of their special-needs children and all that can be learned and gained from a life of caring for a special-needs child.

The Connor Principles are designed to help parents and their families cope with and manage the issues that will come at them on their journey. They're designed to help caregivers find new strength and inspiration to reframe their situations and move forward with a renewed energy, grace and understanding, spirit and purpose—both at home and at work—*reducing* their own *level of stress* and *anxiety*, and that of the families as well.

My goal with this book, future books, the *Weekend Caregiver Summits* and our work through *The Reach For Me Network*, is to take better care of the caregivers so they are emotionally supported and empowered to care for their special-needs children, and feel better about themselves and their future in the process. The world community needs to become more aware of, look up to and honor the courage, conviction and selfless humility of caregivers for their unending emotional and physical care they give these children day after long day. I know of these emotions, struggles, stresses and challenges firsthand as a caregiver.

Another goal of this work is to create a global dialog and much deeper level of understanding and compassion within the numerous constituencies directly impacted and that *intersect* around the issue of caring for special-needs children: employer organizations, schools, the healthcare establishment, the life insurance industry, banking, financial planning industries, the legal establishment and justice system, the pharmaceutical companies, state and federal government programs, etc. They *all* need to understand at a deeper level the continuous hills and valleys of the caregiver's heart, mind, spirit and finances along the way. There's an inner peace that can come from what these angels from above teach us, which, as I am learning, can deepen the meaning, purpose and joy within our own lives.

By offering this story about my situation and sharing the continuous journey we caregivers are on and the principles I've come to learn from my son Connor, I hope you will feel a warm blanket of support from your extended family and friends as you go about your daily lives of providing care and attention to those who require much more of you because they have special needs.

I pray you experience a deep peace in your most challenging hours, with grace guiding your thoughts and actions as you learn to care perhaps on a deeper level, and cope with the situations that have entered your life's path.

I hope this book also inspires those who are dealing with a sudden or life-changing situation calling for massive strength and understanding just to hold things together as you cope with the host of emotions coming at you all at once (e.g. the loss of a child or spouse, job loss or change, sudden news of an illness, depression, anxiety, despair or a general uncertainty about where your life is

3

headed). I hope the principles I've learned from my cognitively challenged son will allow you to become more open to what the principles are really about, helping calm and center you as you look for a deeper meaning and purpose in those moments when you wonder if anyone cares or understands.

Open your heart as you let this true story and the principles that have come as a result of my life situation, experiences, ongoing learning and hardships, help you in your everyday life to find a deeper meaning so you too, can keep moving forward.

Be well, and move forward.

—Michael A. Boylan

A MESSAGE FROM CONNOR

(In Connor's Voice)

Hello. My name is Connor, and I am [a] special-needs boy with my father; his name is Michael. I like doing the blower all day, sometimes every week and weekend, playing my drums, being in the jazz band, listening to music, and talking to my paraprofessional. And I want to be in the marching band in school pretty soon.

My dad is 23 years old** and I am 16 and in the 10th grade at Chanhassen High School in Chanhassen, Minnesota. Special-needs children are important because they were born beautiful. My sister is a basketball coach. I love her. She is my sister. I know sometimes it is [a] hard life. Sometimes, people get hurt, but it's going to be okay. I wish you the best you can [be] with your special-needs child. They are like me and we are special children from the Lord. Have a nice day! I hope you will like my book about life. Thank you. Peace out!

—Connor M. Boylan

**I wish!

Connor enjoying a jazz concert on the hill in Snowmass, Colorado

Signing up for first day of camp at Challenge Aspen Music and Dance Camp

I have learned that writing is a gift often requiring the talents of others experienced in editing and preparing a work to be of value to others. It is with genuine gratitude that I therefore wish to thank the following people for assisting me with this work: Megan French for her cover design and layout expertise; Wendy Burt-Thomas for her talents around copyediting and readability; Peter Lanpher for his expertise around print production; Robert Boylan, my father, for his many photos, which are contained throughout; my mother, brother and three sisters for their encouragement through the dark and visionless years where I couldn't see anything positive ahead; Father Bob White and Father Arnold Weber for their counsel, especially over the past five years; Dick Rice for walking with me every week—always ready to lend an ear; and other friends who encouraged me during the tough years—more of which are more than likely ahead.

I also want to thank in advance the media personalities who will interview Connor and me, helping foster a greater awareness of the millions of caregivers of special-needs children throughout the country and around the world who continue to give their lives for the well-being of their special-needs children. Remember, it's not a good thing if caregivers just give up and throw in the towel. In that scenario, we all lose! The caregivers, their families, the special-needs children, and **all** of us. In this scenario, we'd all pay the consequences through **higher taxes** to fund more federal and statewide assistance-related programs. It's *common sense*, therefore, that we understand the scope of what's going on around us when it comes to the far-reaching implications of this issue on millions of caregivers, the companies who employ them, governments and societies.

Finally, I want to thank the one above for putting the song *Angel Child* into my head while jogging one cool fall morning in Minnesota, during a particular low point. It came so fast that I had to sit down at the piano to play what I was hearing in my head: a song inspiring me to write and arrange for an orchestra, then record with a full orchestra, professional choir and many special-needs children and their parents.

Thank you to all the musicians and singers involved, mastering sound engineers, mixers, arrangers and videographers who shot and edited the music video for *Angel Child*. They captured the emotions that need to be conveyed about what it can be like to be a caregiver of a special-needs child. Purchase the *Angel Child* song and music video on the website listed below, or on the iTunes store if you haven't already, and you may find a deeper level of understanding and compassion for those in your own community who are caregivers to a special-needs child. **Order details** for the anthem song *Angel Child* and music video and *The Making of Angel Child Behind-the-Scenes Documentary DVD* can be found by visiting the website at **www.ReachForMeNetwork.com**.

Nowadays, many of us are so busy, stressed out and wound up about all the important *stuff* we must deal with from one day to the next. Hence, we're all tight on time and want to know *right now* how this or that could help us, so we can decide where to invest our time, knowing the payoff will be there. Therefore, let me address that issue right now.

If you are a **parent** or related family member caring for a special-needs child, this book was written for you and can help you. Credible research and various articles report that as many as **one** in **five** families in the U.S. is directly or indirectly involved in caring for a special-needs child, which, if you do the math, means as many as **35 million** people in the U.S. alone are impacted and touched by a special-needs child. Globally, the number of caregivers impacted is even larger. A sizeable community of people who are dealing with emotional, physical, financial, psychological and spiritual challenges of worry, doubt, frustration, anger, anxiety and despair on some level, fairly regularly as their special-needs children grow up. Hopefully, this book will give you some comfort in knowing that you are not alone, but in fact, are part of an expanding global community of gifted people who've been *called* for an extra level of service to our children.

If you are going through a job loss or change, the principles in this book can also help you through your transition period. And, if you are coping with challenges with your children, friends, coworkers or boss, these principles provide a road map for arriving at resolutions, helping calm and center you, as you make sense of all the shuffling around you.

If you are searching for more balance and want a framework to help you resolve or handle the tough stuff that comes up throughout our lives, these timeless principles will endure. No trendy advice here, but rather principles full of common sense, dignity and genuine respect.

Life is difficult at times because *people* can be very difficult, self-absorbed, overly fascinated with themselves and unbending at times. I don't think this is negative thinking, but rather just a fact of life. It's a truism that we're all going to happen upon various speed bumps on the road of life. Sometimes they are downright miserable, but with time, things can come back. However, there are other speed bumps that cause *permanent* changes, where things might *never* return to the way they were. And for certain, these permanent bumps can seem unfair, overwhelming and very unsettling—as if your compass for the right way forward doesn't exist anymore, forcing you to figure things out on your own. In these situations, who doesn't need some help or a little pick-me-up once in a while, or reassurance that things are somehow going to work out, even though all you might feel at the moment is confusion, despair, anger and total disbelief?

We all have moments when we wonder, *What the heck is going on? Why is this happening to me? Did I do something to deserve this? Why am I not catching any breaks? Are things going to get any better, or am I being punished?* These are all questions I wanted answers to ASAP when the sudden permanent news and events hit for me. But the answers didn't come that fast. Maybe that's the case with everyone. Or maybe in the waiting, we are being *shaped* and *prepared* for other purposes down the road that we have no idea are ahead. Nobody has a crystal ball, though it sure would be nice sometimes.

During our lives, most of us will go through at least four sudden, unexpected, significant events or changes in our professional and personal lives which, when they happen, tend to impact *everything* over time. When these things occur, we know there are three basic choices we can make:

1. Do nothing, tread water, mope, become angry, bitter and effectively paralyzed to take any type of action—my case for years.
2. Go backwards, allowing the psyche to fixate, causing people and organizations to retrench and lose ground, or they can …
3. Go forward, dealing head-on with the circumstances, digesting, understanding, reframing and finding new inspiration to move forward with a

fresh perspective; allowing us to get past the tough stuff, becoming reenergized to take on the road ahead with a renewed spirit and sense of peace, to be of better service to others—in my case, to my special-needs child.

When traumatic things happen, the old expression *"this too shall pass"* just doesn't cut it for many folks—especially when the things happening are *permanent* changes to your personal and professional life—events that will impact your life forever.

In these times, trendy, temporary *fixes* will not suffice. We must rely on a set of **guiding principles** that can bring some level of peace and calm during the storm, helping pull us back up, out and forward. This is the simple power of *The Connor Principles* ™—principles that have application in personal and work-related situations; a common framework for dealing with challenging situations for the betterment of all involved.

What's unique about this book is that it's a **true story** about how my life changed instantly and forever with the birth of my special-needs son. There were no warnings, no preparations and no guideposts to follow, leaving me feeling alone and full of anxiety. It's also about how our family came *unwound* with the struggles and hardships that took place as a result of learning to cope with new life pictures, pictures which had never entered my mind until everything hit all at once. It changed and eventually destroyed the relationship between my wife and me. It impacted the relationship with my daughter and our friends. It affected how we lived on a daily basis, coping as best we could while trying to learn how to care for Connor and handle *life* and work at the same time—a continuous challenge to this day.

I share the struggles and challenges of a new life with a child that needs me to be present in the truest sense—mentally, emotionally and physically—and how it *forced* a reordering of everything; work, travel, business relationships, friendships, attitudes, activities, my faith, beliefs and feelings. And the constant fight within that is part of the process of trying to understand the questions I kept asking myself: *Why me? Why am I being singled out for this? I have no ability to do this! What the h… is going on? Who's in charge here? How am I supposed to get anything done in life?*

I offer these emotions, which I have struggled with, as honestly as I know how. I'm sharing my challenges as a single father caring for my special-needs son, as well as the process of total *surrender* to his needs, and the deep peace it has brought me in times of total confusion and despair.

Please understand that this is *not* a cry-in-your-beer, self-directed sob story. Instead, it's the truth about how this new life challenge pressed up against and challenged everything I had learned as a young man, forcing me to relax, chill out, open up, let go, and trust more than ever before that somehow things would be okay around this new life I am learning to adjust to as I write this book. I am learning a brand new way to deal with and be grateful for the challenges that are, at times, overwhelming, yet have also enlightened me and many others. And believe it or not, they have made me a more complete person, and a better helper of others, because I have a deeper level of understanding. It's as if an *angel* has been standing next to me the entire way, an angel child named Connor.

The Connor Principles™ are my lessons from a cognitively challenged beautiful son who has taught me more about life—and what it's supposed to be about—in a few short years than anything I've learned through schooling, athletic competition, business, friendships, my church or just living. The principles are meant to serve as a **living guide** in those times when your world seems totally upside down and nothing fits, nothing is in order, and your attempts to bring things under control don't have any positive outcome—at least within the timeframe in which you wanted relief. They've been such a help to me since I was raised as an organized, can-do, motivated person focused on staying on track. And yet, I now ask myself, *Whose track?* Because that style of living doesn't work for Connor. As a result, they've helped me learn how to change, serve and remold my personality to accommodate what my son needs. That has been challenging, but ever rewarding.

11

My sincere desire is that you will use these principles in your time of need so you have less stress, less anxiety, a deeper peace and a gentle grace guiding your thoughts, emotions and actions as you deal with the challenges that have entered your path of life and work. Let this story and principles find their way to bettering your life.

—Michael A. Boylan

Connor Boylan,
my teacher

Enjoying the music at a rodeo
in Snowmass, Colorado

Reach For Me

THE STORY OF MY SON CONNOR

TABLE OF CONTENTS

The Story of My Son Connor

Table Of Contents

All of us compare our *situations* to other people's situations and often determine how we feel about ours by comparison. We look to see if anyone's got it is *tough* as we do, or has as difficult a life. I do this, and I know parents of specials-needs children that do this as well. We *all* do. Some more than others because it can be very lonely when you are the primary caregiver and wonder if you'll hold up, just for that day. I don't know why we're like this. Maybe it's our way of coping with our feelings, frustrations and fears, by comparing ourselves to who has it better or easier than us, to those who've got it much worse. So that our pain, sorrows, confusion and anger are justified in some respect.

When my situation hit, I truly felt as though I was the only person in the world dealing with such a difficult emotional and challenging road. I didn't know if I could handle it, or if I had the depth of patience, temperament and ability to earn a living while being a committed caregiver for my son. Could I be emotionally present for him in the manner he required for his progress and feelings of self-worth, since his spirit is *so* sensitive emotionally? These were huge things for me to learn, and I am still learning them.

Parents and families of special-needs children are a unique and special community of people who have been handed lifelong situations that are not only challenging, but also very hard emotionally, psychologically, and sometimes spiritually, day in and day out, because they cut to the *core* of what we are about really—our children; what we want for them and for ourselves. And it challenges many of the early life pictures and expectations of what *we* want out of life. Sometimes, it deals us life-changing news so hard to accept that it takes a lifetime to adjust. Perhaps it's similar to someone suffering from depression, anxiety or another life illness or situation, such as an addiction to drugs or alcohol, or work.

Based on my experience of giving, and giving, and giving care, love, total focused attention and a calm heart to my son, there are days when I wonder if I have anything left to give to anyone else. And then I wake up and do it all over again the next day without acknowledgement, which is what I mean when I say I am learning how to surrender and serve. Special-needs children require this selfless humility. And if you can't give it, it's very easy to become permanently depressed. The challenge for me moving forward is to feel lucky and blessed by the joy that comes from serving my special-needs child, Connor Michael, the angel child that's been given to me for a special reason.

Seeking attention is *not* my intent in sharing this story. I have been led to share the things I am learning from a cognitively challenged son who has no idea that what he is teaching me may be the very essence of what life was designed to be about—that everything somehow is going to work out and be okay. And that I've been given *the* most beautiful gift; the opportunity to learn how to love, serve and receive love from a special-needs child who only understands how to give, and isn't waiting for *anything* in return—and to understand that *this* is serene peace.

AND WHO ARE YOU? —A SMALL BACKGROUND IF I MAY

If anyone would have told me that at 54 years of age I'd be writing a book like this, I would have said *"No way, totally impossible."* But I never expected or even thought about the circumstances that were about to come upon me back in the early winter of 2000/2001 when my son Connor was clinically diagnosed with *Williams Syndrome*—a time that will always be *cemented* in my memory as if it happened yesterday.

Born the first of five children, three sisters and one brother, to proud and committed parents, I was brought up in an entrepreneurial family where hard work, self-determination, self-reliance and dedication were not only important, but also the way in which you were supposed to *be* as a person. These attributes were important to nail down, shall we say. Being a self-starter was perhaps most important of all, if you asked my father. Get up, get dressed, have your plan of attack, then *get moving.* I think I was around 7 or 8 years old when he gave me my first full-blown Day-Timer calendar so I could begin learning to manage and prioritize my time. Got the picture? An organized, taskmaster father who believed that accomplishing the task at hand and then moving on to the next one was not only an important lesson, but also the real *core* of how to become successful in life. This bit of information is important since this *pattern* of living, burned into my head since I was a child, would be challenged head-on to its very core when my son was born.

We were by no means financially well off as a family, but we never went without in terms of anything we needed. We didn't take airplanes on family trips, as there were seven of us; it was the wood-paneled Chrysler station wagon loaded down to the max. We had plenty of food and nice clothes, went on summer driving trips to Colorado, Canada and northern Minnesota, and always had the athletic gear we needed for hockey, tennis, baseball, water and snow skiing, and the other sports we participated in. Looking back, life was good and I felt lucky. Childhood was a good and happy time.

My wonderful mother, in addition to being a stay-at-home mom, also taught French and English at the local middle school a few blocks from our house. Since I can remember, my father was self-employed in the advertising business, so we were used to dinnertime discussions about how things were going; new clients, clients who were leaving the firm, and general concerns about building a small business. We enjoyed family camping and skiing trips, and all of us were competitive athletes. Swimming, baseball, hockey, tennis, water and snow skiing were all part of learning about people—and life.

My father, always the taskmaster of the family, made sure that we all chipped in and did our chores on a regular basis whether we wanted to or not, contributing to the family's well-being. Chores often came before homework, hockey or baseball practice or sporting events. We got decent grades in spite of all the major projects around our 110-year-old house on the lake. The house actually had old newspaper stuffed in the walls for insulation, as we learned when we began to remodel, one area at a time.

Aside from the typical sibling infighting, I had a loving, safe and happy upbringing. I learned that if you wanted to get anywhere in life, you'd better be diligent, work hard, stay focused and remain upbeat throughout the hills and valleys of life, because they were going to happen (just never to me; for sure, never to me!).

Church was an important part of my upbringing as well, and we went to the local Catholic church. Between my experience as an altar boy and influences from my aunt, a Carmelite Nun for 45-plus years, I was raised to believe in and revere God.

However, all of the things I would learn in my early years were going to be tested and challenged to their core much later on—in spades. So much so that, at times, I didn't know if I could live by them anymore, or if they were just for other people, but not for me.

Aside from playing competitive hockey, tennis and baseball since I was a kid, and keeping a B average in school, my first brush with the unexpected came on March 26, 1979 at 5:50 a.m. on an interstate highway headed west for The University of Montana in Missoula. I was returning for spring quarter as a college freshman. My parents let me take the jeep for the spring quarter.

After driving from Minneapolis to just outside Billings, I couldn't stay awake any longer, so I pulled over and asked the person riding with me, who'd been sleeping for several hours, if she felt okay to drive. About 5:30 a.m. we made the switch. Twenty minutes later, she fell asleep behind the wheel and veered off the highway. The jeep rolled end over end twice, according to the trucker behind us who witnessed the accident and stopped to help. The force of the impact almost dropped the engine out of the jeep. I was thrown out the back of the vehicle a couple hundred feet. She was pinned in by the roll bar with just a few missing teeth, but went into shock soon after she was helped out, probably after seeing me.

I lay on the highway, my waist and legs on the pavement, my mouth full of blood and gravel, my left hand pointing in the wrong direction, I couldn't move my legs, and I was working hard to get enough air.

With a smashed left wrist and 90 percent compression fractures of lumbar one and two, I had broken my back pretty badly, a half inch from being paralyzed from the waist down according to the doctors in the emergency room. Thankful to be alive, competitive college hockey and tennis were now history. No way would contact sports ever be an option for me again. After being flown back to Minneapolis, I began a three-year recovery process of constant rehab and therapy, wearing a custom-made metal brace from my neck to my waist, which helped me stand and balance as I learned to walk again. The brace was the substitute for what they used to call Harrington Rods, an option the doctors at Mayo Clinic offered as another avenue of treatment if the steel brace didn't work.

After finishing college around therapy sessions, I got a job with an international nonprofit educational and musical group called Up With People, traveling and securing funds for and promoting large-scale events. Being involved in the half time entertainment for Super-Bowl XVI at the Pontiac Silverdome in Detroit, and working with senior executives of large firms involved in sponsoring big events was great business experience.

At age 26, a business partner and I started a technology-oriented distributorship serving multinational clients in the banking, credit card collections, outbound telemarketing and receivables management industries. Years later, we founded a second firm, providing background credential verification services to large employers. Life was getting back on track.

Thirty-one, single, and caring for my father's mother who had the beginnings of early stage dementia, I sold my ownership in both businesses and struck off into the music business. I recorded several tracks at Prince's studio, Paisley Park in Minneapolis, with the best of musicians, hoping to secure a recording contract with one of the major labels, but to no avail. There was no recording contract, lots of red ink, and a dwindling savings account after two successful ventures. All of a sudden I felt unsuccessful; my first major-league failure.

While putting the pieces back together, I met a woman several years younger with a beautiful 2-year-old daughter. We married a year and a half later, and I eventually started my next venture, a management consultancy launched with the publishing of my first business book through a major publisher in New York. Years later, a second book followed, and a third book was published in 2007.

Managing to grow the business amongst the tumultuous times after the dotcom disaster, the telecommunications and technology slowdown, 9/11, and the financial shenanigans of senior officers at several large firms engaged in fraud, was ultra challenging, to say the least.

In the midst of building a life for my family and me and all the ups and downs that entails, my wife (now ex-wife, I'll explain) announced she was pregnant and that we were going to have a baby in August 1998. Excited and nervous at the same time, the overriding anticipation of our first biological child together was a peaceful thing to think about. The preparation and countdown for a new baby began.

CHAPTER TWO
WHAT MAKES YOU SO SPECIAL?

Absolutely nothing. I'm a proud father who, like many others, works hard to provide for his family so they have what they need throughout life. As an entrepreneur of 25 years with all the fits and starts that that life can bring to keep clients happy, the cash flow somewhat stable (as clients file for bankruptcy, stiff you and lift your intellectual property), and relationships strong, I was managing pretty well on all fronts. I've always liked children, so having a biological child was exciting, and made me feel lucky and full of pride. I would work on being the best father I could be and focus on giving my new child and my daughter the kind of upbringing that I had. And of course—if it was a boy, then we would do it all! He'd play hockey, baseball and tennis, just like his dad. We'd do all the cool stuff that only dads and their sons can do together.

CHAPTER THREE

PREPARATIONS FOR HIS COMING—
HOPES, DREAMS AND EXPECTATIONS

There was so much to do to get ready! Getting the baby's room painted, crib and mobiles set up—we were all on standby for the big day. As we were preparing, all of these pictures of what I wanted and assumed life would be like with a new child came flooding into my mind—pictures of what I wanted to do with him (if it was a boy), where we'd go together, the things we'd talk about and experience as he grew. I wondered if my thoughts were similar to the pictures and feelings a mother has when she quietly hopes for a girl, so she can do all the special things with her daughter that her mother did with her. Of course, I would have been happy if we'd had a girl. But if it was a boy, we could do it all—and we would. My daughter was so much fun—so active, energetic, athletic and happy—that having a son with the same attributes would make us the complete family I had always envisioned. One beautiful and talented little girl, and a new baby boy. Maybe.

I didn't understand where all these thoughts and expectations were coming from, but they were clearly in the forefront of my mind. As if I were in charge of the whole thing from the moment my child was born until he or she got married. No doubt about it: we were going to do *all* the things I had dreamed about with my new child as if I could paint on a canvas just exactly how things were going to go from day one. I had it all planned out. It was like candy being offered to a child, as if I could reach out and select *just those pieces* I wanted for my child and me. Looking back now, I can say how unbelievably *selfish* I was in preparing for my child's coming, focusing on what he would do with his daddy and what he would someday become.

And nowhere in this maze of exciting expectations was there any picture, any thought or any doubt that we'd have anything but a healthy, happy and *normal* child. Nowhere! The thought never entered my mind. Hopes, dreams and expectations are so important in helping us to keep pushing forward in life. But these same pictures can also create lots of anger, sadness and feelings of utter hopelessness and despair, as they did for me, when you realize that the expectations you had so firmly planted in your head will never be met—ever. I was about to learn this lesson firsthand and suffer the deep sorrow that comes and goes as a result—a host of emotions, anger, disappointments and frustrations I would need to learn how to handle and deal with moving forward.

I can't speak for anyone else. But to act as I did, as if I were in charge of the entire event—from birth throughout my child's life—was a harsh awakening that *someone else* was in charge of the whole thing. And here I thought my hands were firmly on the wheel and that I was driving the bus! I think it's a classic flaw of sorts with an entrepreneur type.

What I couldn't understand at the time was that I was setting myself up for a feeling of hopelessness and despair so deep that I didn't know if I could ever climb out of it.

CHAPTER FOUR

THE PERFECT SON—WE WILL NAME HIM CONNOR MICHAEL

I stood at the side of the bed next to my wife like the dutiful husband, keeping a cold cloth on her forehead as the doctor and nurses swirled around her bedside debating whether an epidural was necessary. Everything was moving very fast.

The hospital room was buzzing with medical staff barking directives rapid fire as I attempted to keep her comfortable. I was actually panicked. I had never gone through anything like this before. This was our first biological child together and everything was new to me.

I wanted to update my mom so I peeked out the hospital room door, finding her in the hall. I told her what was going on and that it might be a while before the baby was ready to come. Being a spiritually connected woman, she walked down the hall and began to pray, as she typically does in times of great need. Within about 10 minutes, the baby was ready to come. The doctor and nurses were amazed and I was freaked out and nervous, and feeling in the way.

Then, all of a sudden, the baby started to come. There was no crying, as I remember. A quiet baby, and a boy! Six pounds six ounces. They scurried him off to a corner of the room pretty quickly to be cleaned and checked over because the cord was wrapped around his neck, as I recall. After he was all cleaned and put in a blanket, they presented him to us to hold. The most precious gift I have *ever* been given. I stared in homage at my firstborn son and held him as gently as I knew how. I couldn't hold in my tears. I had *never* felt this way before. I couldn't speak. He was so peaceful.

We had picked out a strong Irish name as a symbol for the strong boy I knew he'd become, Connor Michael. I was overcome with a deep sense of peace as I made the sign of the cross on his forehead. He was a *blessed* boy now, though he was yet to be baptized by Father Arnold. It was all so amazing and spiritual. I stood straight as a tree, holding my new son and feeling that now, more than ever, I would be an even better provider as he was going to be denied *nothing* in life.

When we brought him home from the hospital, the normalness of a busy home life with a newborn began, probably not any different from anyone else's crazed life with a new baby. But early on we noticed a major intolerance to milk and lots of crying, different from how calm and relatively quiet he seemed in the hospital. But then again, he was just a baby, so this was all normal, right? Nothing to sweat or worry about. I had a new son, and this was just life with a newborn.

But the crying continued. Lots of crying. As I recall, my wife felt the crying might be a little more than normal, and so did I. Plus, he wasn't eating very much. At seven months old, he still hadn't gained much weight, and after numerous doctors visits (and what looked like a large "outy" belly button), it was determined that Connor needed a triple hernia operation. The doctors seemed to agree that maybe the reason he was colicky and in so much pain was because of the little hole under his navel. As he breathed, we could kind of see his intestines moving underneath his belly button. That *must* have been hurting him so it needed to be addressed.

The doctor at Children's Hospital did an amazing job on the surgery, though I was a nervous wreck during the procedure. To see our 7-month-old in the recovery room in his little hospital bed, all bundled up in a blanket with an IV in his arm made me feel helpless again. But with a successful operation, we anticipated he would begin to eat more over time and finally start gaining some weight. (His head seemed pretty small.) I felt relieved that maybe things would get better— that he would start eating more, have less gastrointestinal problems, and maybe the crying would lessen when we brought him home from the hospital.

But this was not to be. The crying continued. We bought the most expensive baby milk on the planet (something like $5 a can!), which I purchased by the caseload. It seemed to be the only kind of milk that Connor could digest. This helped some, but he still wasn't gaining much weight. We decided to take him to see additional pediatricians and specialists who all ended up saying about the same thing: Not to worry, he's just got some type of bad acid reflux. They told us to cool it on the milk and other dairy products.

The advice was hardly comforting because he was clearly still in pain. We were starting to wonder if anyone could help us find any answers so he could be comfortable. We were exhausted, maybe a bit on edge, and my wife needed a break. I suggested she go to Scottsdale with my sisters to get some rest and relax in the sun.

I took the week off from work so I could stay home with Connor because I didn't trust anyone to watch him other than my wife. It was just Connor and me, all day and all night, for what I recall was about six days. And *then* I understood. I understood how uncomfortable he really was. How much he cried. How I got no sleep. How he'd spit food right back at me when I'd be feeding him. How he'd try to smell anything and everything before it entered his mouth and if the texture of the food didn't seem right to him, or if it entered his mouth the wrong way or whatever, I'd get it right back. And how he'd wake up in the middle of the night several times to cry … and cry … and cry. It hurt to hold him as he cried, knowing it seemed there was nothing I could do other than rock him back and forth in my arms, gently rubbing his head. I was beginning to wonder if I could handle it. It was never ending.

The stress and constant worrying was getting intense. Even though I was trying to keep calm, we were getting no real answers as to why he was so uncomfortable. None! And we were going to good doctors. I worried nonstop, which was not my nature. It was not the way I was raised to be. Maybe some men can handle this level of stress without any problem, but I was beginning to have difficulty and I knew it. I was consumed with so much doubt and fear that I couldn't focus on *anything* except Connor. I began to view my work as an inconvenient hassle, though I definitely needed the income. And I had a hard time keeping my emotions from spilling over into decisions I needed to make to keep the business moving forward. We were living in America with the supposed best health care system, but it wasn't working very well for our son.

There were days while my wife was deservedly relaxing with my sisters in Arizona that I didn't get out of my pajamas. I held Connor constantly, rocking him back and forth. His discomfort continued and my stress level continued to rise, as it seemed nothing I did brought him any comfort. I felt helpless and hopeless, as if we were on some deserted island with all the medical experts saying, *"Gee, I'm sorry, but we don't feel there is really anything that out of the ordinary with your son, though we understand that he's uncomfortable."* My wife and I believed differently. He was in more pain than seemed necessary and we were not going to stop searching for ways to help our boy, until we found something that helped.

The days became longer and lonelier, and we became more isolated, not seeing our friends like we used to because there just didn't seem to be the time to really enjoy them. Being consumed with Connor made it hard to focus on anything else. Besides, we probably weren't that much *fun* to be around either. I can only speak for myself, but I was wound pretty tight, worrying about my son all the time. Perhaps others felt we were too *heavy* to be around or that we couldn't relax or loosen up, which was probably correct, but sad when you think about it. And though I'd begun to hear that these kinds of family situations and stresses could take a toll on any marriage, it had yet to occur to me that our marriage and personal relationship was becoming an unspoken series of deep sadness, fear and hopelessness. There wasn't much laughter in the house anymore, as I recall—no joking, and not many smiles. Except for my daughter's enlightening presence, love, energy and continued accomplishments in the classroom and on the basketball court, life was becoming an unexciting, serious, never-ending grind.

I felt like my head was locked in a vice grip, cranked as tight as it could possibly go. *Nothing* made me smile. The worry never let up. And for a guy who'd been raised to have a positive outlook, I couldn't see *anything* positive ahead. My mind was in a thick fog and I had no idea if it would lift anytime soon. I had never envisioned that life could be this hard. Never! My personality was beginning to change to that of an introvert bracing for the next round of bad news about our son. *Maybe I should just stay in my foxhole*, I thought. There's only so much one can take, right? The perfect son? Yes. He was our beautiful little boy. But he was in pain and there was nothing I could do. And *that* was not the perfect situation for our boy.

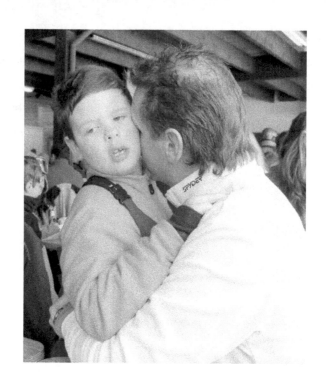

CHAPTER FIVE
HE'S NOT TRACKING, IS HE?

Lots of people have a common way of describing situations by putting them into two basic buckets. Maybe you do the same thing. People say you're either *on track* or *not on track*. Those who aren't on track are usually working pretty hard to get back there. And while we all like to simplify situations to this extreme, as if it's that easy to get back on track at will, I was definitely *not* on track, nor was our son—and we knew it. My career also seemed off track, like it was sliding right through my hands, as it didn't seem to be nearly as fun anymore. My head was so heavy and out of focus on the deals I needed to close. Everything seemed totally upside down, with one of the two most important people in our lives suffering constantly and we were right there with him, suffering and searching for answers and help, but none were coming. There appeared to be no relief in sight, though we tried to keep a good "game face" on as we pressed ahead. I attempted to put a hopeful spin on our attitude toward life and the circumstances in front of us, since we were both fighters. But the *fight* was getting old and tiring. There wasn't much gas left in my tank.

After Connor's first birthday, we intensified the doctor visits, as I remember, becoming even more proactive with the medical community. We asked more questions—to the point of being a pain in the rump to the doctors and specialists. But frankly, we didn't care. This was our son. We listened to every shred of medical advice we got about what other things might be medically wrong with Connor Michael. Deep down we felt he wasn't tracking, but we never really talked about it that much during our alone time, which was almost nonexistent (except for talking about it to and from doctor visits). It was almost too painful to discuss, though we both seemed to know or anticipate what the other was thinking. It was a hollow sadness as black as a bottomless pit—a silent fear that it could be something serious, though we tried to remain positive as though the next day would bring news of possible answers. Something would come, we kept telling ourselves, and it was *just* around the corner.

Hope was all we had. But to be honest, being hopeful was a tall order for me. Like I said, my parents and grandparents taught me to be positive and never lose hope. This was ingrained in me since I was a boy, so I knew how important it was to look on the bright side of things. But *Mr. Positive* was becoming *Mr. Full-of-Doubt*. I couldn't smile if you promised me ten thousand dollars. It wasn't in me. I was filled with sadness. It wouldn't go away, and I couldn't stop worrying. I felt like a walking zombie. This was not like me. I couldn't focus on my work, my wife or even our daughter in the way she deserved with all of her activities—just on Connor. *That* was the proper focus, I thought, even as my business began to slide, as did thousands of others nationwide that were having problems after the dot.com disaster and the attack on the World Trade Center, which caused thousands of companies to shut off spending and go into a foxhole and wait.

Almost overnight, corporations froze spending on *anything* and *everything* that was even remotely related to sales and management training and strategic consulting, the field I'd been in for several years. But even *that* wasn't nearly as important as my son. I almost didn't care much about anything except the health and welfare of my son and daughter. And right now, my son came first, damn it! So why couldn't clients cut me some slack? Couldn't they show me a little compassion and understanding in a family-related matter? Or *at the end of the day,* as clients love to say, is it ALL just about the dollar? It sure seemed like it, because the empathy wasn't there: lots of glowing verbal comments, but nothing to back it up—just lots of "fake" concern.

Who was it that said that in times of great struggle, you learn who your *real* friends are? And whom you can count on in times of great need? This helped fuel my feelings that we really *were* all alone.

I would get up in the middle of the night, go downstairs and cry so I wouldn't wake up my wife. The sadness was thick, deep and heavy. Our relationship was dying and I think we both knew it, though it wasn't discussed much (to my memory) other than comments or short bursts that we needed some counseling or something, which neither of us seemed to do anything about. We were just too busy and so focused on Connor.

We were like platonic college roommates. No time to concentrate on each other's needs or wants because we were both focused on Connor. And I was certifiably sick and tired of hearing people tell me in their soft, even-tempered, calm voices with their tender puppy-dog looks, as their heads would cock to the left, *"You know, God never gives you more than you can handle."* That statement was total bullshit, in my opinion, because he'd just given us that in spades! And God? Where the HELL was *He* in this whole thing? That was a great question for which I had no answer. I felt totally abandoned by Him, though I'd been raised to believe in the almighty creator, and was an altar boy to boot. But why in the heck had *He* given me such a crummy life of pain, never-ending fear, doubt and hardship? It was more than a little hard to be a trusting and loyal believer when all of this constant hardship had become my life! Perhaps I was being punished. It sure felt like it—and for what?

I had absolutely no flipping idea how I was going handle it! I felt stranded and alone! I think we both did. Not to mention, I couldn't focus correctly on my corporate clients and their demands. It felt as though they were badgering me, though I know they were just being clients. I wasn't designed to handle this. Didn't the *man upstairs* know this? It felt like I was coming apart because nothing was making any sense and *nothing* was on track. And for a type A guy who likes having things line up and be in order, this was not a good thing.

Life wasn't supposed to be like this. I knew of nobody around me that was going through these kinds of hardships. I was tired of trying to bring things back on track because nothing I was doing for our son, or for our life, seemed like it was working. Things were so old, so hard and such a grind all the time. People would say, *"He's just not the same guy anymore, you know? Everything is always so heavy with him, don't you think? It's like he just can't loosen up."* That was hard to hear. But the truth is, there are many people in this world who really *aren't* interested in helping. You learn this when your life seems to be in shambles. There are few who really lend a hand.

The medical tests being recommended to us seemed more elaborate as we pushed on for answers; an EEG (an electroencephalogram—a brain scan), an EKG (an electrocardiogram—a quick glimpse of the heart waves), more and different kinds of blood tests, additional meetings with his everyday doctors, gastrointestinal professionals advising different types of foods, specialists looking beyond gastrointestinal issues, and on, and on and on.

Have you ever been in the waiting room of a hospital or specialist's office in the middle of the day (after filling out all the insurance forms, which can make you feel as though they're going to take your house if they don't get their money)? It's not a good feeling; all alone, while the rest of the world is out working away and getting ahead in their lives while you are at the mercy of doctors, who are, of course doing their best, but are also very BUSY. They've got others they need to see right behind you. It tends to make you feel a bit helpless at times, and off track.

And while all these professionals were attempting to be reassuring, it seemed they too were perplexed and tentative, as if they weren't telling us everything they thought. But we were probably paranoid because we were desperate for answers. We picked up on their unspoken concerns, and it was hard to discuss between us. My growing fear was that nobody would be able to tell us anything to help our son. And he *still* wasn't tracking.

I could see the sadness in my wife's eyes, a depth of loneliness that isn't cured with *date night*. As the man of the house, I did my best to hide the same fear. We were tired, I was scared, and our son was hurting. No one seemed to know or have a handle on what was going on. How could it be that some of the best medical doctors around couldn't figure out what was going on with our son? They were the experts! It didn't make any sense to me, and as a result, I was becoming withdrawn. I believe my wife was too. We were all by ourselves on this one. Not fair. Not fair at all.

Little did we know that the pediatric neurologist we'd seen a year or so earlier had a hunch about Connor, but it was never shared with us. Evidently, he had ordered a specific blood test called *The Fish Test* that was never performed by the lab. Somehow there was a screw-up and the test was never done. We found this out a good while later.

What we did understand was sadness—deep, long and unending. *How much of this were we supposed to take?* I would ask in my prayers. *I want some answers, damn it! Talk to me! Is this going to be our life?* Searching for medical answers hadn't told us anything so far. I wondered if we were in for a lifetime of uncertainty while we put on a *happy face* for the rest of the world, which only wanted to talk about happy things, good news, success and getting ahead. Our life was not happy. At least that was my opinion. It was a grind, steel on steel with no end in sight.

The volume of correspondence between doctors, specialists, hospitals, the health-care provider and others grew by the month. Being the organized one— or so I thought—I began a card file and filing system to keep things straight. It was a project worthy of outsourcing with all the moving parts. Which doctors are where, which ones have moved to other hospitals and clinics, who said what, when, etc., and the continual changes from the insurance provider regarding who was in-network versus out-of-network, what they did and didn't cover, which changed frequently. I didn't go to college for this, but a semester could easily be designed for all of this bunk—a task to keep things as current as possible for our boy. We were not going to give up—no way. That was not in my nature, though the thought had crossed my mind more than a few times.

I couldn't remember the last time my wife and I went out for a quiet dinner or just a walk in the neighborhood. What was *that* like? And it felt as though we'd never do it again. And romance? Forget it. It was the last thing on my mind actually, hers too probably, based on the lack of touching and intimacy between us. It felt like the last time we'd even kissed—I mean really kissed— was years. I wish I were exaggerating, but for us, this was our life.

Some of my buddies would joke around when we were in private calling me, "Mr. Once a Semester." They thought it was hilarious, yet it wasn't funny at all to me. It reminded me all the more of how far off center life had become. You could have put a one-foot square wooden beam down the center of our bed and neither one of us would have gotten any slivers. Intimacy was a distant memory as we hunkered down for another long and cold Minnesota winter of no answers, not knowing how to help our son. Maybe we would hold hands—maybe, in the car on the way to the next doctors appointment, with Connor quietly in the back seat all strapped in, his soft, gentle little face staring out the window sensing where Mommy and Daddy were taking him next. It seemed like he was starting to learn where we were going. Another doctor, another hospital, another specialist, test or analysis. When were we going to learn something conclusive about our beautiful little child?

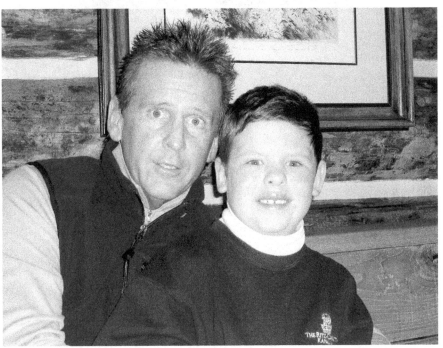

CHAPTER SIX

THE NEWS

With more time with doctors and still no answers, we went along with all the continued tests being recommended, hoping they'd reveal something. We'd done the things they'd suggested, but still nothing, except more tentativeness from the medical professionals. My level of confidence in doctors was dropping like a rock. I didn't understand how the "experts" couldn't figure things out. *"What's the benefit to keep doing all these tests?"* I would ask, and then get back this look from the doctors as if we were total irritants because of the litany of questions we were asking. But I recall them being tentative and they couldn't hide it. They too were confused, and this made us feel all the more nervous and alone.

There was one test we had yet to do because, as I recall, no one had yet brought it to our attention—an echocardiogram, an ultrasound of Connor's heart. It shows the blood flow of the heart. I didn't understand the relevance of the test, but if it could shed some light on things, we were all for it. So we said yes and scheduled the test.

We booked the appointment to have the procedure done at Children's Heart Clinic, one of the finest in the Twin Cities. The highly regarded doctor scheduled to see us happened to be the co-founder of the clinic, an amazingly kind and compassionate man.

It was late fall of 2000 with another Minnesota winter just around the corner. Connor had just turned two a couple of months earlier. The day was cloudy and brisk—a day burned into my memory as if it happened just yesterday. The highway was bone dry, cold and windy. It felt like the first snow was not far off, just quiet and still, with no one on the road; a day reserved just for us.

We got Connor all bundled up and I loaded him into the back seat of our SUV, getting him all strapped in and comfy with Snuffy, his purple blankly, as we drove to Children's Hospital and Heart Clinic for the procedure. Like every other trip to various doctors' offices, I don't recall us talking much, if at all, as we drove downtown to the clinic. Like so many other times, it just seemed easier not to talk, as all the possible scenarios went swirling around in my (and probably my wife's) head about what might be coming next.

I remember how cold and gray it was that day. As we got closer to the hospital, Connor seemed to sense where we were going. His face just had this look. Every time we'd bundle him up and put him in the car he'd clutch me so tightly as if to be telling me, *"Daddy, hold me,"* as he dug his fingernails into the side of my neck like he didn't want me to let him go.

After the routine sign-in process with the myriad of insurance forms, which needed to be filled out each and every time as if they'd never seen you before, we were led back to one of the waiting rooms with lots of children's toys and told the doctor would be with us shortly. We grabbed some toys to keep Connor occupied and distracted from where we were, though based on the look on his face, he seemed to know where he was. We'd been to *so* many doctors and specialists, but we sat patiently waiting. We held Connor and the toy, which seemed to occupy his attention for all but a few seconds.

A sharp knock on the door broke the nervousness and the doctor came in, a warm, kind, interested, friendly man. After the introductions and niceties, he sat down, grabbed his clipboard, looked at Connor intensely, and then looked at my wife and me, back at Connor, then back at us, and within a few seconds his entire demeanor seemed to change. It's been said that in times of intense trauma, people who experience the very same event will recall it, or describe it differently—or take away a totally different memory of what actually happened, even though they went through the same thing. Therefore, I don't know how my wife would recall things, but this is what I remember from that day, which replays itself over and over in my mind.

"Question to you, Michael. Does Connor look like you—or does he look like your wife?" The way in which he asked the question, quick and direct, made me a tad nervous.

"I don't know really," I responded.

"Let me ask again," I recall him saying in an even more firm and direct tone. "Does your son look like you—or your wife?"

"I don't know. I guess me, but he also has some of my wife's features too. He's only two," I said.

The doctor became more intense, but maintained a professional demeanor. He asked some additional questions related to other tests, doctors we'd seen, and then said something to the effect of, "Look at Connor's forehead. Look at his lips. Do you see the elfin features in his face? I think Connor might have WILLIAMS SYNDROME. Have the other doctors not seen this? Just a minute. I will be right back. I want you to read something in a medical journal. Be right back!"

He left the room quickly and I was numb. *He has what? What is Williams Syndrome?* Everything stopped. The room was spinning or maybe it was just my head. I began to cry. I don't remember what my wife was doing. My mind was racing a hundred miles an hour. We had never heard of *Williams Syndrome.* No one had ever brought it up. What was Williams Syndrome? It sounded serious based on his tone and the way in which his demeanor changed so quickly. I'm sure he was being as professional as he knew how, though it appeared he was surprised as well. Waiting a few minutes seemed like hours as I grabbed a box of nearby tissues to dry my eyes.

The doctor reappeared with a thick medical journal opened to the place he wanted us to look, asked us to read the page, then left the room again to prepare for Connor's echocardiogram. I held the book open staring at a bunch of words as tears dripped onto the pages blurring my ability to make anything out. *My son has something called what? This is my son! And he has what? Is this permanent?* I couldn't hear anyone talking to me because nobody was talking to me—just my mind asking a million questions all at once!

I stared at the heading WILLIAMS SYNDROME but couldn't read. I just stared and sobbed. I don't remember what my wife was doing. But I recall staring at Connor as he sat quietly on the floor playing with some toys, oblivious to what was going on in the room. Just peaceful and content, as if everything was going to be just fine, while Mommy and Daddy were struggling to understand the magnitude of what they'd just been told by a world-renowned specialist who was trying his best to be calm, compassionate and professional—all things he was doing well, as I remember.

The doctor returned a few minutes later and explained what Williams Syndrome was, and that there were some signs that indicated, at least to him, that Connor might have Williams Syndrome. We sat there glued to what he was telling us, as if it were so surreal that it just couldn't be happening. The slow-motion movie of our life was beginning and *we* were the principal actors.

"Has Connor had a brain scan—an EEG*?"* the doctor asked.

"Yes, I believe he has," I said.

"Who did the test? Where was the test done?" I recall him asking. As we struggled to answer, he barked out another question. "Has the Fish Test—The Fish blood work test, has that been done?"

"We don't know, I don't think so, but I don't know," I responded. "He's had lots of blood work, but I don't know if he's had the Fish Test."

"And who did the brain scan?" the doctor asked. When we responded, he acknowledged that the doctor who did that test was good.

I couldn't be polite any longer. "What is Williams Syndrome?" I barked. "What does this mean? What is going on? What does Williams Syndrome have to do with the procedure we're about to do?"

The doctor became fatherly and began explaining in terms we could understand as I tried to keep my eyes clear; I don't recall if my wife was crying or not.

"Now, I am not saying conclusively that Connor has Williams, but he seems to have some of the symptoms and attributes of a child with this very rare condition, in my opinion. Basically, if Connor has Williams Syndrome, he could be missing between 20 and 24 or so genes around chromosome number seven. And this gene deletion or inversion, as it is sometimes called, impacts Connor's cognitive growth and general abilities, his emotions, his fine and gross motor skills, his sensory abilities, potentially his heart, which we might see shortly with the echocardiogram, and other areas, such as gastrointestinal issues, etc. Children with Williams often have elfin features like Connor has. Some in the medical community who have heard of Williams refer to it as having some similar traits to children on the autism spectrum, or mentally retarded or challenged. Williams is very rare, discovered around 1997, I believe. The Fish Test is the specific blood test that we know of that helps confirm the diagnosis, which is why he should have the test. And when we do the echocardiogram shortly, if Connor has aortic stenosis, which is a narrowing of his aorta, this is another symptom that would also point to the probability that Connor might have Williams Syndrome."

I probably don't have the correct order or the exact words as to how the doctor shared the information since I was in a trance when he was speaking, but this is what I remember. The conversation was moving too fast for me and all I could focus on were two words; MENTALLY RETARDED. He was saying that my son was mentally challenged, and this meant *forever*. Forever! I couldn't get my head around that concept.

The doctor continued on, as I recall. "Typically, many children with Williams will have a narrowing of their aorta coming off the heart, causing the heart to work harder than it should have to, to pump the blood through this narrower passageway. The echo procedure should be able to show us if Connor has aortic stenosis, which would need to be corrected—if pronounced enough—with open-heart surgery at the appropriate time. Again, I'm not saying conclusively that Connor has Williams, but I have seen a few other children with Williams and it's my hunch that he may have it. I will advise you to go and see a world-renowned doctor at the University of Minnesota after we do the Fish Test and know what that tells us. I believe he will be able to give us a more conclusive diagnosis of Connor since he's renown for studying syndromes of the head and neck in children. I need to get prepped for the procedure now. The two of you can stand on either side of Connor as we lay him down on the table to do the echo."

The doctor left the room as we sat in silence, staring at Connor for what seemed like hours. A nurse appeared to give Connor a liquid sedative to drink, and the doctor reappeared and said it was time. I picked Connor up and carried him down the hall to the room where the nurses and doctor were waiting. My wife and I tried to calm Connor as we laid him on the cold, hard table in this dark corner room as they hooked up the various electrode-looking round rubber pads on Connor's chest. He gripped my hand while trying to pull off the rubber pads as fast as they put them on his chest. Eventually, we were able to get them attached and the test began, Connor fixated on a Teletubbies video on the monitor above.

The room was dark and quiet as they began the test, our eyes fixed on the monitor that showed Connor's heart pumping. As the doctor and nurses talked back and forth, we listened intently to see if we could understand anything they were saying.

"Mommy and Daddy are right here, Connor," I whispered. "It's okay, Connor. We're almost done. Just a little bit longer, Honey." We stared at the monitor waiting to hear the doctor say if he had aortic stenosis.

Images flashed by so fast we didn't know what we were looking at, or what to look for. We remained silent waiting for the doctor to tell us something as Connor kept saying, *"All done? All done?"*

We stood silently, hovering over our son, waiting for a sign from the doctor. And then it came. He looked at us and said; "See this area here on the monitor?" pointing at the screen. "This is where the narrowing is in Connor's aorta; something that can be corrected with routine open-heart surgery at some point. We will need to keep a close eye on Connor as he grows, his weight, blood pressure and other things. Probably once a year, I will need to see him to monitor the situation to determine if and when we'll need to correct it with open-heart surgery."

"So does he have Williams Syndrome?" I asked.

"I cannot give a conclusive diagnosis at this time, which is why we should send all the medical records over to the doctor at the University. You two should go see him to confirm the diagnosis after we run the Fish Test. But more than likely, he may have Williams. Let's finish the echo and talk more in the other room."

Routine? Open-heart surgery is routine? Are they nuts? Open-heart surgery is *not* routine. Not in my book! I rubbed Connor's hand as they slowly took the rubber pads off his chest, wishing that someone would comfort me. I was numb. We put Connor's clothes on, picked him up and carried him back down the hall to the room where we began. The doctor came back in.

"Here's what I think we should do. We need to schedule the Fish Test, which will give us more information in regard to whether Connor has Williams. You can schedule the test here at the hospital. After the blood work is back, I will review it with the neurologist who saw Connor, and we'll talk again at that time. And if the blood work indicates that he might have Williams, I would advise you to see this world-renowned doctor at the University of Minnesota I mentioned earlier. I know him. He is a retired orthodontist but has been studying syndromes of the head and neck in children for years and is published extensively on the subject. I feel he could help us in diagnosing Connor based on what the blood work looks like, okay? Let's schedule the Fish Test and I will call you after the neurologist and I review it, and we can determine if we should send the files over to the University for another opinion."

Everything the doctor said came into my mind in slow motion as we tried to keep Connor patient. We shook hands, walked down the hall, scheduled the blood test, and walked to the parking garage without saying a word to each other, as I remember. It was surreal. I lifted Connor into our SUV, strapped him in, paid the parking fee, and drove home feeling as if we were now in some very sad movie. I don't recall looking at my wife as we drove home, just the road. It was *so* cold outside, dry, quiet and still. When we got home, I don't think we told anyone the news, not even our daughter. We had dinner, gave Connor his bath, which usually calmed him down, and my wife worked with my daughter on her homework or something after Connor went down.

I remember sitting on the bed in our master bedroom, staring at the wall feeling numb and hopeless, as if all the wind had gone out of my sails and the ocean was still. If I tried to be optimistic and comforting for my wife that night, I don't remember it. All those *pictures* of *my perfect life* with our son flashing through my mind in warp speed—almost too much to bear. My mind was being tortured.

My wife and I didn't speak much, as I recall, when she came into the bedroom. We stared at the wall attempting to digest what we had just heard. I would *never* forget this day. This was not supposed to happen to me, not to Connor, not to our family, and not to us. The spiral was beginning. I was in a trance, as if we were all alone on some island with no compass and no clear path to follow. No life raft, no one to help us or hold us. I didn't know what to do, and I couldn't turn off the tape in my mind that kept playing over and over again, *"Your son has Williams Syndrome! Have the other doctors missed this?"*

Connor got up the next day and I couldn't focus on anything. I might have taken the day off from work, I don't remember. Or maybe it was the weekend. I just wanted to be with him, to hold him, look at him, put my cheek next to his and feel his warmth. I had to be with him. He seemed so peaceful and content without a care in the world. No fear, just a peace that Mommy and Daddy were going to take care of him. But I needed someone to take care of me, and tell me that somehow, everything would be okay; that Connor's future and our family would be okay, that our marriage would endure. And that our LIFE was going to be okay! But no one was there to do that, and we didn't know how to help each other. My wife was probably trying to cope with the news as best she could, though I was too slammed to ask. All of a sudden, Mr. Positive, Mr. Can-do, Mr. Take-Charge, Mr. Conquer-That-Mountain, couldn't see a path forward because there was no path, just a thick fog and a feeling that we were sinking into quicksand. Not a good thing for a self-employed entrepreneur that's supposed to have a *happy face* on when meeting potential clients! I didn't think I could do that any more. I felt overwhelmed, filled with sadness and fear.

I don't remember when we told our parents the news, but I remember *all the questions* coming back from them and my brother and sisters, for which we had no real answers yet, because we didn't know either; nor did the doctors, really. *Everybody* wanted detailed specifics, timelines, how severe Williams was in comparison to things like Down Syndrome, Autism, Tourette Syndrome and mental retardation. *Exactly what was Williams Syndrome? How long would it last? Would he ever outgrow it or was it forever? What does his lifespan look like? How much extra outside help would Connor require throughout his life? Would or could he ever get married, have children, drive a car or live on his own? Would he for sure need open-heart surgery, and if so, when? What would the surgery accomplish? How did this happen anyway? Was this a genetic fluke or did my wife or I have some gene or abnormality that we passed on to Connor? Is Williams some new discovery in the medical community? Because we've never heard of it. Just exactly where does he fall on the Williams scale of severity?* And on and on and on. The more questions, the deeper I sank into despair because we didn't have any answers. All the questions kept forcing the tape in my mind to play back, *"Your son has Williams Syndrome. He is mentally challenged."*

All of these questions, plus tons more, were the same ones we were asking the physician. Unfortunately, we didn't have any answers yet, because they didn't know for certain either. We were in uncharted territory, which made me feel hopeless, like we were being punished. This wasn't supposed to happen to me. Not to Mr. Full-of-Hope. My life was supposed to be happy, fun and successful—meeting exciting people, traveling to new places with our family and living a normal life, whatever that is. But these things were sliding away, as if I didn't deserve them anymore, replaced with a deep coating of life stress, intense anxiety and pressure surrounding my first-born son and what seemed a permanent medical diagnosis we'd have to learn about, understand and manage to live with for the rest of our lives as best we could.

At Sunday Mass, I held Connor as if it were the last time I'd have him in my arms. My head felt like it weighed 200 pounds as I knelt in the church pew asking God for a sign that things were going to be all right somehow. I wanted to know what was to be gained in all of the sorrow and shock. But nothing came. I wasn't getting anything back. Ever felt like God has turned on you? That you've gotten a raw deal or the shaft? That He's not listening? That you're all by yourself? I had no comfort, just a cold feeling of having to find the answers on my own. This didn't track with what I'd learned about faith, grace and patience growing up in the church.

December 2000 brought us a quiet and lonely Christmas as I remember. It was just family, as we didn't feel like going to holiday parties. I don't remember celebrating with friends, or shopping for gifts. I think we ordered most of them from catalogs that year. We put the tree up, though I don't know why, because it didn't feel like there was anything to celebrate. Everything was hollow, cold, quiet and lonely.

After Christmas and New Year's Day, it was back to the grind. I was trying to be positive at work but not doing a good job of it. We waited for the results of the blood work, grasping for a sliver of hope that maybe the doctor was off his rocker and didn't have a clue about what he was talking about. *Maybe he was totally off base and Connor didn't have Williams Syndrome.* I tried to hang onto these thoughts, but they never lasted for more than a few minutes, as I was becoming an accomplished pessimist. I knew the doctors we'd been seeing were top notch, and the likelihood of them being way off was remote.

Sometime in the new year, the hospital called to say the results of the blood work were in. We booked another appointment to talk with the doctor about what the results from the Fish Test showed. On the day we drove to the clinic I was attempting to be hopeful. As I put Connor in the back seat and strapped him in with Snuffy, (which he likes to talk to because Snuffy is a real person to him), he had this look of total serenity on his face. A calmness that Mommy and

Daddy *knew* what they were doing, that we *knew* how to care for him, that we'd be there no matter what. It was a total peace, trust and calmness that pierced through me and made me cry. I made the sign of the cross on his forehead, getting him situated in his car seat. He loved sitting in the back of the Navigator like King Tut, looking at everything from his perch as we drove downtown again, hopefully to hear good news—a development—something to hope for instead of what we were expecting to hear.

My wife's hand was cold and limp as I reached out in a gesture that everything would somehow be okay, while my mind raced with scenarios of life moving forward. I put on some classical music, which always seemed to calm Connor as we drove to the place we'd become all too familiar with, Children's Hospital and Heart Clinic, on another wintry Minnesota day.

The mind is a powerful thing. So powerful that when you get bad news, news you don't want to hear, it can block you from consciously remembering specifics because it's just too hard. I can't honestly tell you how the doctor told us the news, or, the exact words he used. Just that the blood work was positive indicating Connor more than likely *did* have Williams Syndrome—the *gene deletion* around chromosome seven, and that we should forward all the blood work, along with the other test results, over to the specialist at the University of Minnesota for a second opinion. We called to schedule an appointment to see this new specialist as soon as possible, which took more than a casual effort since the guy was in semi-retirement and finishing research for his third or fourth book to be published by Oxford Press in London. In addition, he was battling a permanent health issue of his own. We finally got the appointment several weeks out.

On the drive home, if my wife and I talked or tried to comfort one another, I don't remember. All I remember is staring straight ahead at the road, looking at Connor in the rear-view mirror all calm and serene, wishing someone would give *me* that kind of peace, because I felt like collapsing. My heart was broken. I had nothing more to give and didn't think I could hold up under the sorrow

49

of not knowing how to handle all the news, uncertainty and sadness. It was traumatic to hear that Connor's situation was LIFELONG! *What was I supposed to learn from this? And why me? Why me, and my family? Why my first-born son?* This is was too much to bear.

I could feel my relationship with my wife moving further and further apart—sliding deeper into our own little cocoons to digest and process what was happening, and hunker down. The stress of caring for Connor, figuring out what we were supposed to do next, and the uncertainty that was ahead was enough for me to consider throwing in the towel and giving up. This was just plain raw, hard and endless. There was no peace in sight for the Boylan family—none, just more stress and uncertainty. The news had come, and though we'd yet to get confirmation from the second specialist at the university, I was certain he'd confirm the findings. In my mind, we already knew the answer, and it was *permanent*.

51

CHAPTER SEVEN
WHY ME? WHAT AM I SUPPOSED TO LEARN FROM THIS?

I was a God-fearing, former altar boy, and a church-going, hard-working and trustworthy family man. What more was I supposed to do to *prove* to the man upstairs that I didn't deserve this? I mean, at the end of the day, as all my business friends loved to say, "What the hell? Wow, man ... you've got some serious stuff to deal with. I am very sorry to hear the news. No offense, but I wouldn't want to change places with you, man. I don't know how you do it."

Not exactly marvelous words of comfort, though they were probably doing their best despite their confusion about what to say. This was part of the problem, in a sense, because the news was so intense. No one knew *what* to say. What was there to say? When you learn of news that is overwhelming, that comes out of nowhere, what *can* you say? Some people retract and say nothing out of fear they'll say something dumb or out of sorts. However, we probably couldn't hear anyone else anyway. We were in a state of numbness. At least I will speak for myself, as it's never safe to assume you know or understand how another person is interpreting the same traumatic situation, even your spouse.

I don't know how most people handle traumatic news because I'm not a therapist or psychologist. And who knows if we went through the *typical phases* of the grieving process, but I could really care less. I was numb, angry, exhausted, sad beyond words and tired of it all. I had had just about enough, thank you very much! It felt as though God was trying to single me out for whatever reason, and I didn't appreciate it—not one bit; not for the life I was trying to put on the boards. I was being *picked on,* in my opinion, harassed and interfered with. That's how it felt. Another *speed bump* in my life, only this one was major league, much more so than my car accident when I broke my back and ended up in a metal brace for years. Connor's diagnosis was *permanent! Forever!* I couldn't fix it or change it. This was hard to digest, that I couldn't *fix* or *solve* the situation. I had to learn how to handle it, live with it, change my life accordingly, and find some peace with the whole thing, though that's not where I was at the time. I was angry, pissed off, sad, scared, lonely and paralyzed. I had busted my butt for way too many years getting my company launched, my first and second books promoted at the national level on CNN, Bloomberg Financial and others, executed a nationwide book tour, trained multinational clients on the methodology I'd developed and written about, kept a roof over our heads, paid for the extras like nice family vacations, kept my daughter's private strength and conditioning training going (since she was becoming a very talented basketball player), and all the other things that make up everyday life!

To say I felt as though the wheels were coming off the train would have been putting it mildly. I was tired of the daily grind of it all, and the definitive news about Connor put me over the top. There's only so much a person can handle before they wonder if they're going to shut down, and I was there. I was sick and tired of people tilting their heads to one side and saying in their soft little voices, "*You know, the Lord never gives us more than we can handle,*" or "*This is right where you're supposed to be right now.*" Well I am sorry, but what the hell does *that* mean? Yes, I'm a God-fearing person, but honestly, how are these comments to be digested when you are sad beyond words? When you're at your wits' end, grasping for anything that can help you make sense of it all? I wanted answers from the one above, and felt I deserved them … right now! Was God trying to break me down, or something? It sure seemed like it. In fact, for a while, I became convinced I was being broken down to nothing, and He was doing a marvelous job of it. At one time, I thought maybe I was *wired* to the top, being the good Catholic, Church-going, family man, and an aunt that's a Carmelite Nun for goodness' sake. Doesn't *that* qualify for some level of special graces? But this wasn't buying me any points as I kept asking for signs in short order. *At least* I deserved that much, since *He* was giving me a boy with profound special needs.

Being a small-business owner for twenty-some years, I wasn't into this concept of *"find some quiet within yourself"* holistic mumbo jumbo. I wanted a billboard on the highway telling me *why* this was happening, and what I was to learn from it. The pressure was so great that I felt entitled to some answers. Why was I *picked* for this hardship? Was I some guinea pig selected to endure this level of pain, sorrow and helplessness? And for whose benefit? I kept asking what could be positive in all of this, because based on my assessment, *nothing* was positive about the situation—nothing at all! I kept praying for answers but nothing was coming, which made me even more scared and depressed. A stunningly fabulous combination of emotions to have when attempting to grow a business in a difficult economy, putting forth that positive outlook necessary to win business from clients who don't *care* about your personal situation, as sad but true as this really is. In point of fact—remember this: I made the grand *mistake* of sharing in confidence, the news we'd received about Connor a year or so earlier with one particular client, who I thought was a heartfelt guy, only to learn after sharing the news that his company was now "concerned" about my level of focus on their account. What a hell of a note! *Guess I can't trust sharing the news with anyone except our closest of friends*, I thought. A friendly world we live in, isn't it? When people *need* some solace, and what you get instead is a totally self-absorbed response that sends a clear message that they couldn't give a rip!

The more I prayed for answers, the more isolated I felt. I became more introverted, as I wasn't getting any peace. My personality was changing, and this started me down the path of questioning the value of my faith, the core of what I'd been raised to believe since I can remember. Life wasn't fun anymore. And my son had a lifelong diagnosis.

*What do you **want** from me? Haven't I been a faithful servant? I need help understanding why this is happening to me. I don't have the emotional capability to handle a special-needs child, let alone the money for everything he'll need over the course of his life! Why me? This is not funny!*

This was part of my prayer life, if you want to call it that, but nothing was coming. No peace, no comfort, and nothing was letting up, just more stress and anxiety. And Connor *needed* me. He needed to know I was right there, and so did my family. And as cold and unending as everything seemed, giving up was not an option—though I thought about it a lot.

Looking back, I can now understand that nothing was happening *to me,* though this was exactly how it all felt at the time. In fact, to be honest, it felt like I was being persecuted in some manner, or tested for something that was to come, though I had no clue as to what that would be, since what I'd been doing for the last several years fit my talents well. And though I didn't have the emotional depth or understanding at the time, the most special of gifts was being given to me, though I didn't comprehend or welcome it. I was just mad, sad, scared and confused. And I needed help, but I didn't know what I needed, or whom to ask. Life was cruel and I certainly wasn't getting any breaks. It was hard to be anything but sarcastic toward the faith I'd been raised with, since it seemed to have all but abandoned me.

There was no love, comfort, or understanding coming, yet I had to muster up a new level of patience around something I didn't understand one bit. I wasn't a caregiver by nature, in fact, who is? Think about *that one* for a minute! Who grows up saying, *"I want to be a caregiver"*? Something *extremely* hard to do for most of us, and it doesn't come with any sort of training manual. But I was going to have to learn how to become one by trial and error because this was what my son needed. That's what I would have to become. A caregiver. I'd have to learn how to adopt a new temperament and new level of patience. This was going to take awhile. I'd need to learn a new calmness, and a new level of trusting in my higher power since everything was well beyond my control. So much so that even attempting to plan my life or anything related to work seemed impossible at the moment—perhaps even stupid, since *everything* was up in the air. To be there for Connor, I'd have to learn to become a different person, to mold myself into a new personality around what this new life was going to look like, as best I could tell. The fear and uncertainty was intense, but out of survival, I was carving a new charter and a whole new chapter without knowing, basically out of survival.

First year at Challenge Aspen Music and Dance Camp

SHUT THINGS DOWN—TURN OFF ALL THE NOISE

With no sign of comfort, it was time to hunker down and wait to see the second specialist at the University of Minnesota to verify the findings of the Fish blood work test and whether Connor would receive an official diagnosis of Williams Syndrome. Or maybe he'd give us different news—though I doubted it, since these guys were sharp. We needed to be as patient as possible until we saw the other specialist.

I don't recall for certain, but I think we told our daughter, both sides of our families, and the two Catholic priests I'd been friends with for years (one of whom married us) the news about Connor sometime after the first of the year. It was before we saw the second specialist, since I didn't see any sense in waiting. The second specialist would likely confirm everything, so in my mind we already had our answer.

For my wife's and my sanity, we needed to turn off all the noise around us and hope for the best, knowing we were powerless over our situation; not a great feeling for a guy who likes to be in control of his destiny, especially after having it pounded into my head that if you *weren't* in control, you would surely end up with a handful of mud, as they say. With everything swirling around us, we stopped answering the phone—at least I did, reduced the number of parties and outside events we went to (other than our daughter's basketball games), and pretty much kept to ourselves, as I remember. Winter was here—cold, still and lonely. Things were frosting up in my mind. I knew I was having trouble keeping everything going, like my attitude and the travel schedule for clients, which sometimes meant going out of the country to deliver their sessions. I kept feeling like I needed to be with Connor more and more. There were so many balls in the air at once, but all of a sudden, Connor needed to come ahead of everything. The volume of medical correspondence back and forth was on the upswing, and it would only increase as we learned more. A new year was upon us, 2001, with lots of doubts, fears and uncertainty about where life would lead next.

The day we drove to the University to meet with the second specialist, Connor again had such a beautiful peace on his face, that it touched me to my core; a piercing calm over his whole person, like some angel from above, no worries and total serenity—as though he *knew* something I didn't. His gentle, soft cheeks made me feel warm as I lifted him into the back seat and got him all situated with Snuffy. My mind was swirling with how everything was going to work for Connor, our family, our marriage, my job and me. I've never considered myself a worrier, but I was on the fast track to becoming the world's foremost! And how do you keep fear and sadness from showing on your face? I couldn't do it, a hard thing to deal with when trying to convince a new client to do business with our firm. Some people are good at faking it when their personal life is in shambles, but that wasn't me. The concern and worry must have shown all over my face, as business slowed nationwide and internationally, thanks to the beginning of the technology industry meltdown, the dot-com bust and the market's steady decline. Management and sales training-related initiatives were not exactly on the front burner in the executive suites of corporate America. In fact, we were moving into perhaps the worst drought in the sales and management-training industry, which the industry itself didn't see coming. Not exactly wonderful timing for me. I was looking for some breaks, but they were not on the horizon. I'd have to continue to grind it out one deal at a time.

As we entered the second specialist's office, I recall a doctor in his 80s who looked like the mad scientist from the movie *Back To The Future*. He had long, silvery-white hair going in all directions, and was friendly and talkative. The whole package made for a guy that was definitely *way* out there. After exchanging niceties, I began.

"Have you looked at the blood work from the Fish Test and other files forwarded from Children's Hospital, like the EEG, EKG, echocardiogram and other tests?"

"Not really. Don't really need to. I can tell," I recall him saying. He then took over the conversation watching Connor like a laser, as he moved around the doctor's office exploring all the fascinating things.

The doctor began. "When I start talking to Connor in my Daffy Duck voice, I want you to watch what he does with his eyes, and the expression on his face."

Connor reacted just as the doctor had predicted, moving his eyes up and to the left.

"Connor will keep exploring things in my office and eventually find the stereo receiver behind my desk. He'll stop, explore it, and then push the power button on."

Connor did this too! *What was this, some kind of freak show?* I wanted him to look at the test results. That's why we were there—to learn his medical opinion, not watch as he made a bunch of predictions about what Connor would do next while in his presence. I wanted the data and his sound medical opinion about whether or not Connor had Williams Syndrome. My patience was running thin. We'd been in one too many doctors' offices, gone through more tests than I could remember, tried more things that some doctors and researchers thought might help that didn't, and now this guy was talking like Daffy Duck and asking us to watch what Connor did next? This was serious! This was my son, and I didn't feel he was taking our meeting seriously. I had been told that this guy was "out there" but also, whip-smart and highly regarded in medical circles around the world for his research and intuitive knowledge of children with syndromes of the head and neck. He was a specialist of world-renowned stature! But he could at least look at the blood work!

"Doctor, have you looked at the medical reports regarding all the tests we've done with Connor? What is your assessment? Do you think he has Williams?"

The doctor became more conversant as he shared that he had actually reviewed the medical test reports and blood work, and did feel the findings supported the diagnosis that Connor had Williams Syndrome. When we heard his assessment, we began to barrage him with a litany of questions about what to do next.

Since I was resigned to this outcome, and maybe my wife was too, expecting him to agree with the blood work and the other doctors, it wasn't as much of a shock this time, though I don't know what my wife was expecting; maybe the same thing. We sat there humbly as he explained in high-level medical jargon, the *gene deletion* that is the essence of Williams, the typical symptoms on the spectrum itself, and all that they didn't know, (since being discovered in 1997, as I recall him saying, thanks in part to this blood test called the *Fish Test)*. We listened while trying to comprehend what he was saying, since he was a researcher who was challenged to articulate things in layperson's terms.

So, we had met with the world-renowned specialist at the University and had our second conclusive opinion validating what the others were telling us: our son had Williams Syndrome. He gave us the spectrum of, *"Here's the good news, the bad news, and the news we just don't know"* about Williams, which left me feeling that we were definitely in uncharted territory. This was especially true because the medical community didn't have answers to all of our questions, being a relatively new "discovery." But that didn't stop us from asking questions until we didn't have any more. And when it felt as though there was nothing more he could tell us, other than **we were in for a life of unknowns and major challenges**, he complimented us for being committed parents, extended his office as a resource, and coached us to find a good set of doctors that could help us quarterback Connor's care throughout his life. We thanked him as he explained he was battling a terminal diagnosis himself, and that he might not be around much longer, though we were welcome to call him anytime.

I recall thick silence on the ride home. My mind was working so hard it felt like you could hear it winding inside. We had our answer now. A second world-renowned doctor published on children's syndromes confirmed the diagnosis. It was time to turn off all the noise until we could figure out what to do next. I was moving into a state of numbness. Winter, in my mind, might never leave.

I'd been raised to look at the glass as being half full, but wasn't so sure why a positive outlook was beneficial now. It didn't make sense anymore. We'd just been given shattering news about our precious son, my first, and maybe, my *only* son. He was our boy, the boy I was going to play hockey, baseball and tennis with, and watch play high school and maybe college sports. He was the son I was planning to roughhouse with, the son who was going to get married someday and give us grandchildren. All of these uplifting *pictures* housed in my mind for years were now clouded and foggy. I couldn't see them anymore, though they'd been in the forefront of my mind since my wife was pregnant. They were more than likely not going to happen now. And he was just 2 ½ years old.

Ever had your expectations *locked in* because you were *certain* that things would happen *exactly* as you expected, so your anticipation is through the roof? Now, all those pictures were stolen from my mind, hopes and dreams about life with my son now dashed. I needed some time to digest everything—space to comprehend and figure things out. But there was none of that. My family needed me, and I needed to meet the demands of our clients. The time to let things sink in to comprehend the news would have to come in between every-thing else, as life kept moving. And I was starting to shut down.

I CAN'T CONTROL THIS! HOW CAN I SUCCEED NOW? —AT WHAT?

Is **control** a necessary thing to have in order to be successful—control of your mind, your emotions, feelings, actions and your attitude toward life? And what about control over your work and professional life? Isn't *that* a basic requirement in order to succeed? I believe most of us would say yes. It's a grand topic of discussion for men and women alike. I'll come back to this because I don't have the answers to any of the questions, and because it's such a broad area for debate based on whether you're a man or a woman. And your opinions are just that—based on your views and your circumstances. There aren't any right or wrong answers, just whatever you believe to be the case. But it's a *heavy* topic for most people, the issues around control—and control of what? The topic cuts into the very fabric of our beliefs around how we conduct our own lives. It's that deep, and also confusing, at least for me, based on my Christian upbringing, since many claim that Jesus wasn't concerned about control, or success, as he lived a life in total harmony with the Father. And the Bible says He was essentially the most successful person ever, though no one viewed him that way while he was on the earth! Yet Christians the world over celebrate his birth every year in a little holiday celebration called Christmas, and the Bible remains the bestselling book in all of history. And with all that good teaching since growing up a God-fearing young man, here I was—still searching for more control! Perhaps I was missing the whole point of it all!

So you can understand why I was having control issues with my *life* at this point, and wrestling with the issue of why it seemed like it was being wrestled away from me by some force I couldn't get my arms around, slow down, stop or CONTROL! This was adding to my general feelings of helplessness; not a good thing when as a man, society gives you a roadmap that says you're supposed to be *large* and *in charge,* and *on top* of things. At least if you want to be a man, and have the kind of perfect life often portrayed in the media all around us, which says you **must** be in CONTROL if you want to be successful!

Well, I didn't feel in control in any form or fashion, and was beating myself up because of it. I wanted to give up and surrender the fight. I was tired of feeling like my mind was in a vice grip on some workbench, cranked as tight as it could possibly go. But I was still trying to secure that sense of calm, though the harder I tried, the more out of control things seemed to get. I now understand why so many people who are special-needs caregivers, and people going through major trauma in their lives, are in a state of high anxiety much of the time. It makes sense based on the level of constant stress, as there often isn't any *end* to it all, when you are the parent or related caregiver of a special-needs child. The caregiving **never** ends. And what's worse is, so few of us are natural-born caregivers. It does not come naturally to most people—the constant need to be there and be present on so many levels, and to give, give, and give of yourself. Like I said, who among us grows up thinking, *"Hey, I want to be a caregiver when I grow up, so I can deny myself much of what I **really** want to do with my life and care for the needs of someone else."* Think about that one for a minute. And there are over 35 million caregivers out there in the U.S. alone, according to various estimates.

But it's time to be even more honest and say that though I was focused on Connor's needs, I was also worried about my family and what this would mean for our life! It's true that, in many cases, we as a people are quite **selfish** and **self-consumed**, even when life-altering news comes out of nowhere. And I would say I am no different. This is why we need help—others around us who can relate to the stresses, fears and anxieties that run deep, and the emotional rollercoaster of it all. Even when the news is about someone else, such as our son or daughter, we often *first* focus on ourselves and what *we don't have, won't get* or *won't become* as a result of whatever the news is.

Truth be told, this was a big part of what I was buzzing about in my mind. Just trying to deal with how things would work out, not understanding that I could have been more *trusting* that things were going to be okay. But control-oriented folks such as myself want *answers* and we want them now! I had little time for patience since my world was crashing down around me. I felt entitled to answers or at least some level of peace. And since no answers were coming, I thought the best thing to do was to grab control of the situation, which, I realize in hindsight, I couldn't have controlled anyway.

Maybe it's a male thing, but not having control of the situation added to my insecurities of how screwed up and upside down everything had become for us. And that translated, based on my upbringing and mindset, to an unsuccessful person with an unsuccessful life—more depressing still.

My mind wouldn't rest with the potential scenarios about life, work, our family, money, medical insurance, Connor's overall health needs throughout his life, our daughter's needs as a successful budding athlete, etc. And my lack of being able to control any of it was driving me deeper into despair and depression, something foreign to me. Being forward-looking for the sake of being positive felt ridiculous to me now. I was done faking it. I was in a fight for my son's care and nurturing, our family's well being, and the *pictures* ground into my mind subconsciously about what I wanted to do with my life since I was a boy. All of a sudden, nothing was on track. In fact, everything was derailing faster than I could blink.

These *pictures* of the way life was going to be with our newborn son were also going to have to be dealt with somehow as *everything* was now on the table: our future, my family's well-being and my own mental and emotional stability. My wife, from what I could tell at the time, (though I didn't know the signs of depression or high anxiety in her or myself), seemed to be a trouper, dealing with things in stride, maybe better than me. I'm not saying she didn't have her days, because she did. We both did. But from what I could tell, she seemed to be handling things okay, at least on the surface. On the inside, I can't really say, even though we were married. It's much harder to know these things, since men and women are so different in the ways we deal with and cope with anxiety and ongoing life stresses, especially those directly related to your children. In fact, many people say that you don't really know who you are married to, or in a serious relationship with, until something serious happens to your child or children. It's only then that you find out whom you have as a partner, since tough times or a tragedy often reveal the innermost character of a person.

Since we were deeply sad at various times throughout the week, (though from my recollection, we never talked much about it because it just seemed too hard), we seemed to *assume* what the other was thinking or feeling without taking the time to really verify it. Sure, this was a big mistake. I understand that. But in a time of massive stress and anxiety, how many people do you know that actually take the time to see if they're doing everything *by the book,* while focusing on the other's needs and concerns? Nice to consider the textbook version of how to handle tough times, but that's not what we were doing, at least from my perspective. We were trying to deal with what life had tossed our way as best we could. And it's hard not to feel alone, since life continued to move at the same pace. It seemed everyone else's lives were going along quite nicely without much stress or interruption. And then there were The Boylans. *"Hey, did you hear the news about the Boylans' son Connor? Williams Syndrome! Yah, can you believe it? It's just so sad. It breaks my heart. I think it's maybe something like Down Syndrome, or like Autism or something like that. I don't exactly know for sure, but it's major. He is like mentally challenged. I feel so sad for them. He's just such a gorgeous little boy."*

As they say, news travels fast, so as people in our circle of friends and beyond began to hear the news, we were answering questions like guests on some television talk show circuit, clearing up a bunch of misinformation as stories wound out of control about what Connor did and didn't have. We didn't *have* the answers to all of their questions, giving me an even deeper feeling of being out of control and not in charge of our family or my life.

I was moving into a slow-motion setting on the *life* remote control as if I were outside myself looking in on everyone who would come into our life, do their best to express their concerns and support, then move back to focusing on their own lives, as anyone would. It's just that explaining Connor's situation over and over, and then trying to respond to the next round of questions, such as, *"What are you guys going to do?"* put my mind into a thick fog.

Everything was in a state of flux, including my career. I would need to find clients closer to home to reduce the travel, though I would have to take clients in any location for a while, until I could close deals closer to home. I would need to be more positive, which I was doing a lousy job of. And I would need to wrestle with those *pictures* and *expectations* of what life was going to be like for us with Connor. They were going to be different pictures now, though I couldn't yet see any of them.

The permanency of the news took months to settle in. From my perspective, my wife and I began to drift further and further apart, internalizing our sadness, fears and frustrations. The focus on Connor and our daughter came first. Right or wrong, that's how it was, and we were last—not a priority, really. Connor's needs were at times all encompassing, so we usually tended to Connor first, then our daughter, and if there was any time left, we seemed to somehow not share it with one another.

In my opinion, my wife was becoming even more control-oriented, while I was moving in the opposite direction. And since our marital relationship had been sliding in the wrong direction even before Connor was born, the stress from the news about Connor only exaggerated the gaps in our marriage and the lack of intimacy we'd been experiencing. I suggested we see a marriage counselor, priest or *somebody* about our issues. But it always seemed to end in an argument or some version of silence, in which we wouldn't talk for a while, so we never did anything about it. I guess we were both at fault in one way or another.

I don't know how a woman deals with these types of *vacancies* in her life, but I felt unwanted, unattractive, and in a way, not needed or even desired *except* for when it came time to writing a check for something. I *got* that part. In those times, the fake, insincere smiles and plastic hugs came out, a splendid reward. Sometimes I got a peck on the cheek. But other than that, we'd become platonic roommates who might discuss being intimate once in a great while, but only followed through with a handful of times every year if that. I was lonelier in my own bed lying next to my wife, staring at her back, than I was in some hotel on the road while delivering one of our programs. It was a horrible feeling. I was married, yet alone. To be fair, maybe she felt the same way. I really don't know because our communication about *us* was poor and so nonexistent, that to assume we had a good read on each other was crazy thinking because we seemed to move on assumptions more than anything else. Talking about the real issues, whatever they were, seemed too hard now, especially with all the issues we had to focus on for Connor's sake. So, the health of our marriage was put on the back burner … and left there to burn. My resentment toward her increased, and I would guess that hers toward me did as well.

I didn't feel as though I could control anything so I stopped trying. It was the mental equivalent of throwing up your hands in desperation and yelling, "Whatever!"

As the news of Connor's diagnosis sank in, we began engaging various therapists and doctors to chart a course to provide him the services that might help his cognitive, fine and gross motor skills, speech development, sensory issues, nutritional needs, gastrointestinal issues, and other needs, in addition to his regular heart checkups. Learning where to look to find, then manage, all the professional caregivers, their schedules, opinions and personalities was a full-time job we both shared.

Connor would be 3 years old in August of 2001. He was the most adorable little boy with the gentlest peace about him when he was in a calm state. I couldn't get enough of staring at his face and holding him as he seemed so content, peaceful and at ease with life. I *wanted* the calm, inner peace that he had. Life was swirling, but Connor had this calm about him that was alluring. Was he my angel child? Did he know inside his cognitively challenged mind that somehow things were all going to work out okay? I wanted someone to tell me they would, though I had absolutely zero confidence they would. I had the pessimistic thing down quite well now.

On the work side, it seemed my business, which had doubled in revenues for four consecutive years, was poised to double again in 2001. At least I had *one* thing that seemed to be going okay. It appeared we were headed for our fifth consecutive year of doubling our growth, which was going to be significant. It was late summer of 2001, and we had several proposals and contracts awaiting approvals and signatures with Fortune 1000 companies, due to be approved and signed in the coming weeks. That felt good.

I'd wrestle back control of my work life and channel my stress into building the business, which seemed headed for another growth year moving into 2002. I'd refocus the client mix closer to home, as I wanted to spend more time with Connor and my family.

Then 9/11 hit. Almost overnight, no one returned phone calls. The senior people in the companies I'd been dealing with for months went invisible. Proposals and contracts awaiting approvals, signatures and re-ups dragged on, eventually grinding to a halt. Clients and prospects that were ready to sign contracts went into foxholes. Everyone waited. Long-term clients frosted up and no one seemed able to find a phone, or even their laptop to send an email indicating what they were thinking. Just silence. And these were the largest deals I'd ever had. Nothing I had worked so hard to create and close over the last few years was coming in, other than work from existing clients. People turned harsh, rude and *everyone* was classic non-committal. One by one, the deals I was counting on slipped quietly away into the night, never to be resurrected.

Since nobody was returning calls or emails, I learned the fate of one deal in the *Wall Street Journal* with a headline something to the effect of, *"EDS to close EDS University in move to save $16 million."* Magically, our proposal for an initial training engagement of just under $500,000 (leading to a much larger opportunity when the pilot proved successful) wasn't going forward now after 16 months of consistent effort. I learned this as the new year began.

I learned the fate of another client later in calendar 2002 with a call from our banker.

"Hey, Michael. How's it going, buddy? Say, have you seen the front page of the *Wall Street Journal* this morning? You might want to check that out. Isn't that firm one of your clients? We have the signed contract in our files, don't we? Do you think you'll get paid from these folks? This is major. We should schedule some time to sit down and review your line of credit to see how you're situated, as things seem a bit tenuous out there. What's your schedule like this week or next?"

It was interesting timing since Norwest Bank was merging with or being acquired by San Francisco-based Wells Fargo who was centralizing decision-making power, making it almost impossible to get an answer from anyone in the Minneapolis branch. But as banks sometimes do, they elected to call our line of credit, after we were honoring the terms, forcing me to zero it out in short order. I'll never forget that. In my opinion, the only way to truly have leverage with a bank is when you're into them for a ton, so they *must* work with you. In my case, it was a large line, but not for them, and they wanted their money! So they got their money, forcing me to sell ownership in my firm to pull in more cash. And all the while, I was attempting to get settled into a new life of having a special-needs child, learning new medical jargon, new treatment therapies, seeing if they'd work for Connor, dealing with the times when they didn't work, managing numerous therapists and their opinions about certain types of therapies, seeing if there was any impact on Connor, coordinating their availability for treatments, etc. It was overwhelming, but we didn't have another choice, which compounded the feeling that my head was going to burst. How much can one person take before they say, *"You know what? This isn't funny anymore. Is someone trying to tell me something? How much more are you going to give me before I break? Is that what you want? Am I some sort of marked man, or just someone who has the **worst** luck on the planet? Did I do something to deserve all this?"*

I was getting no relief, and I'm guessing neither was my wife—though I am not certain, since our marital relationship was moving into frozen territory. To my recollection, we didn't share our feelings much about Connor, how we felt about the situation, life or each other. In my opinion, we didn't communicate much, except on a surface level about our daughter and Connor's needs, schedules, doctor's appointments, upcoming therapies, basketball schedules, etc. Life was not warm, gentle, sensitive or intimate. It was harsh, cold, and *You're on your own, pal.*

Succeed in this type of environment? At what? I was just trying to hold on for dear life, maintain the business we had coming in and keep everything afloat. But it all seemed much harder now, and much less fun. I was being led around by one situation after another, not knowing where or when the next traumatic situation would hit us. It was taking a toll and I knew it. I was moving deep into myself and away from the quick-witted, happy, high-on-life attitude important to convey to others, since people don't like being with a *heavy!* But that's exactly what I was becoming. A *heavy!* And who wants to be around a heavy? Not too many folks I know.

I couldn't break the sadness and sense of loss that had come over me, even though I knew Connor was getting the utmost in medical care from all the doctors and therapists. I watched my medical insurance premiums climb year after year as they put us into higher and higher *risk categories* due to the increasing number of claims. And there was nothing I could do about it, other than worry about whether they were going to cancel our insurance someday due to the increase in our claims. But on a brighter note, all the doctors and care providers seemed to fall in love with Connor, since he was the most sensitive and caring of children. He was a gentle, soft soul that would let you see right into his heart and he had this genuine curiosity for everything. Everything he focused on made you stop and take a second look, since he was fascinated with the simplest of things.

Because Williams impacts chromosome number seven through the deletion of between 20 to 24 genes (according to researchers at the Williams Syndrome conventions), Connor's brain is not "wired" in the same fashion as what might be considered a normal child's brain. Hence, I might be putting on his pull-up, washing his hair in the tub, feeding him, brushing his teeth, or trying some brushing therapy on his back, and for Connor, though we may have done it hundreds of times, each time seemed as though it was all brand new to him. The genuine wonder and amazement of the simplest of activities around self-care or any other thing, though we'd done them hundreds of times before, would often cause me to pause and reflect at what he found so fascinating. It was as if he was telling me to slow down, chill out and smell the roses. And in those times, when the basic routines didn't—for whatever reason—sit well with Connor and he pushed back on whatever we were doing, I reminded myself that he was not trying to be difficult, but rather just himself. He was doing the best he could. It was another subtle reminder that I was not in control, nor was he, and that we'd just need to find our way together.

Over the next few months, Connor's fascination with the most basic of things, events, happenings and people began to cause a change in me. I began attempting to see or find a new joy, a new pleasure in the simplest of things, events or people. In a sense, he was teaching me a new depth of life, a new dimension of appreciation for the basics, which in some respects, started to make me more relaxed and appreciative. His ability to look at people's faces and intuitively sense if they were happy, sad or hurting, was amazing to me. He would stare at people's faces, and then mirror their emotion with either a smile or a sad face or a simple comment, like "Daddy sad." He was—and still is—amazingly dialed into people's faces and their emotions. His soft, peaceful way made me want to be around him all the time.

I would hunt for business, dealing with all the corporate fluff, pomp and insecurities that suddenly seemed so prevalent that it all started to become quite tiring to me. But then I'd get the chance to come home, take off my suit and hold Connor as he rocked back and forth, rapidly opening and clenching his fists over and over again. I loved to feel his calm. There was no worry, no fear and no unrest in him—just a gentle peace, which I badly wanted. I would often just stare at his face, tracing the sign of the cross on his forehead as I watched in wonder, trying to see what was going through his little mind. There was something so serene about him that impacted my soul. I was running on a treadmill, but challenges at home were calling. I was being pulled in both directions, knowing I had to earn a living, yet just *being* with Connor made me the happiest. It felt as though I was being softened, but for what or why, was not at all clear.

The constant strain of life with a special-needs child continued to weigh on both of us as 2002 came and went. We struggled to find breathing room between multiple therapy sessions, doctor's visits, additional tests, and coping with the everyday pace of life, which seemed to get faster all the time. The news about Connor was still settling in my mind and I wasn't prepared nor equipped to handle it on many different levels; perhaps no one is when you receive traumatic news about your child that is permanent. *Permanent*, as in, *for the rest of your life* permanent! In one sense, it's like a baseball bat to the head—a blow that takes years to adjust to, with some never fully able to adjust. Focusing on work became hard, which was foreign to me. It made me nervous because I understood the need to muster up the willpower to work.

I'd sold stock for an influx of capital so operating expenses and the monthly needs were covered, while riding out the slowdown in the economy as a result of 9/11 and the technology collapse nationwide. Battening down on expenses—both business and personal—became my focus in hopes things would turn around, and that 2003 would start to improve again.

The management consulting and sales training business had been imploding nationwide. One of the largest firms in the country was on its way to becoming half its size in terms of revenues—a sign things were *not* good in the industry. This gave me validation that it wasn't just me that was having a hard time, since one of the largest firms in the country was struggling, angry shareholders and all. But it made me nervous about whether I could make it in the current economic storm. I used the time to write my second book while prospecting for new accounts, and delivering on deals I'd closed. Things stabilized, so our lifestyle continued as it had been. I covered the losses by refinancing the house thanks to the equity built up over the years.

For everything we'd been through, we were holding on okay. Our daughter was making amazing strides in school with her grades, her friends and on the basketball court. And Connor was making progress with all of his therapy sessions, inch by inch.

It was our marital relationship that wasn't advancing. In fact, it was moving in the wrong direction, in my opinion, almost to the point of being dead. But I didn't have the energy or the willingness to dig into marital counseling. It just seemed, right or wrong, that it would be unwise to start addressing whatever was so vacant in our marriage. Even though I was unhappy, and I think she was as well, we had *so* much going on, all of which were priorities. Our children were so important, and Connor needed the lion's share of the attention. It just seemed like it would be best to let it pass and maybe things would improve over time.

I did my best to avoid bringing up the topic of *us*, since we were both tired, wired and often on edge—at least I was, with all the stress from work and home life. And when I did bring it up, which often moved into uncomfortable arguments, I don't think either of us had the energy. It seemed that avoiding the topic altogether made the most sense for the time being. And so it sat there—our marriage, on hold behind everything else, which felt like it should come first. And bless my daughter, because she never seemed jealous over the amount of time and attention Connor needed from me or my wife, a sign of true maturity and an unselfish attitude.

Though things were going along month to month, the constant stress was having an impact. I couldn't smile. I'd see photos of our family over the past few years where my face was expressionless. I'd look at myself in the photos and think, *Where are you? Where did you go? Are you in there? You look like a total zombie.*

I was gone from myself, if that makes any sense. Nothing was fun anymore.

Everything was *one big chore*, a grind from one day to the next. I felt *something* was going on inside, though I couldn't articulate what it was. I was being redirected or repurposed through brute force or by some power attempting to get my attention by grinding my life to a halt, and changing things pretty dramatically. I couldn't understand what was going on. It felt as though something was pulling on my mind, my heart and me.

THANK GOD the clients we had felt our training programs and consulting services were of high value. That kept our heads above water. But the grind of looking for new clients in a scary economic time drew so much energy. I needed to be calm, patient and present for Connor, but it left me drained. Dealing with the corporate B.S. of being told something different by five different people who didn't care much for one another (though they'd put on a great show about how team-focused and committed they were to their enterprise), was all a big joke to me now. It all seemed incredibly fake, especially when I had a needy, beautiful little child to care for, protect and hold.

Trying to convince large and mid-sized organizations that it might be a good idea to invest in helping their sales organizations become more proficient and proactive in a struggling economic period fell on deaf and scared ears. Those who proclaimed they were empowered with the authority to make decisions were nothing more than empty suits hanging on for dear life, keeping their heads down, as they collected their paychecks. Many senior executives didn't know which end was up, so doing nothing seemed to be the right call. Not much leadership in corporate America. I learned that through this period. Just a bunch of big talkers with fancy titles that hang on every word of the highest-ranking executives, who also don't have much of a clue on how to navigate in rough waters.

Due to the anxiety about Connor and the energy I had to devote to him, his doctors and therapists, I was losing my passion for the material I'd developed— something I *never* thought would happen. A mid-life crisis? Maybe. What I *did* know was my engine was running out of gas. My tank was getting lower and lower, and nothing was there to fill it up; not work, not my wife, nor our friends.

And because none of our friends had special-needs children, it was impossible to expect them to comprehend what we were dealing with on a daily basis. When we'd try and explain what a normal day might be like with Connor, they appeared to think we were complaining, so it wasn't worth the effort to share the *real* stuff. It seemed like too much effort. No one was able to relate to the loneliness and the focus required of having a special-needs child. Not that our friends weren't compassionate or sympathetic people; they were. But they weren't living the *life* of a caregiver of a special-needs child, so I couldn't expect them to understand what it was like. So I pulled back from sharing the day-to-day stuff. It was too much work and I needed to save my energy.

The one person who did fill my tank was Connor. I couldn't get enough of him and wanted to be close to him all the time. We met with therapists, doctors and other caregivers to help him progress in all aspects; his eating, his fine and gross motor skills, his sensory issues and overall cognitive development, his hearing, his speech, life skills, etc. It seemed rewarding and worthwhile, not to mention important.

My life had become unbelievably strange. I'd deliver a keynote address to a group of 150 to 1,000 or more business people—6,000 people at the Microsoft World Fusion Conventions—about the material I'd developed, receive a standing ovation, only to then feel totally alone and under accomplished. *Nothing* made me feel good or accomplished *except* when I was with Connor, caring for his needs with all the others helping us on his behalf. How weird was this? Not feeling accomplished after receiving a standing ovation from thousands of successful businesspeople? What in the world was happening to me? This was not like me. At the end of the day, it felt like it was just Connor, my daughter and me, since our marriage showed no sign of thawing.

Succeeding had been ingrained in me since I was a child. And though we were living in a nice home on a five-acre lot, with nice clothes, nice cars and nice family vacations, I didn't feel one bit successful. I was engulfed by the fact that I now had a special-needs child to raise and take care of—perhaps until I died. I worried so much that I was certain others could see it on my face. It was impossible to relax, and making sure Connor was getting what he needed, along with my daughter, was about all I could handle. All of a sudden, I was unsure about the direction in which I was headed. That was a *bad* thing, since I'd always been clear on where I was going. Now I wasn't sure about any of it. It was one day at a time now.

Though our marital relationship felt so surface, we both took our responsibilities as parents seriously. And since everything seemed out of control in one way or another, this gave me the feeling that I could do *something* right. I took pride in the fact that I was involved mentally, physically and emotionally with my wife at many, if not most of, Connor's therapy appointments, understanding what they were doing and why, the doctor's visits, appointments and tests. I was also present at home when I wasn't on the road, which, at its height, might have been nine to 10 nights a month. In comparison to a senior executive with a major corporation, I was traveling much less. I was involved in Connor's morning and evening care routines. I wasn't the kind of father who sat on his duff watching television or reading the paper while his wife took care of everything. I was there, trading off giving Connor a bath, feeding him, taking his pull-up off and getting a fresh one, getting him dressed and undressed for bed, putting him down, etc. We were good caregivers. It's just that Connor got the lion's share of our attention due to his needs and luckily, our daughter seemed to understand why. Another sign of her inner maturity and strength.

Though I was struggling to close deals in a horrible economy, I managed to keep all the balls in the air, but barely. It was enough so that my wife didn't have to work outside the home if she didn't want to. But to keep her sanity with some outside interests, she did have a job off and on during some of the years of our marriage.

I was getting more satisfaction from caring for Connor than anything at work, and felt good about it. Control was sliding away from me at work, but there was someone who needed me at home. And since we started this chapter talking about *control* and being in charge of your life's direction, I remember one particular story like it was yesterday.

It was one of the *first* telling times where I felt like I might need some help dealing with all the stresses swirling around in my head, though I didn't know what kind of help I needed. I just knew I was going dark.

I think Connor was six when, on one particular morning, I was scrambling to get him showered, fed, clothed and bundled up, so I could put him in his car seat and drop him off at this Montessori Morning Care program for a bit, not far from our house. My wife and I felt this place was great for Connor, because of how focused the woman was with him. I was getting Connor fed and ready to go so I could drop him off, and carry on to my appointment in downtown Minneapolis. I was hurrying, something hard for Connor to comprehend or do. There is no such thing as needing to hurry, as it doesn't register with him; drying him off, putting on a fresh pull-up, brushing his teeth, washing his face, putting his clothes on gently so he wouldn't feel rushed, getting his socks on exactly so, so they weren't bunched up in the toes (which would cause him to fixate on his feet and then we'd have to stop everything until his socks were just right), feeding him some breakfast, cleaning him off again, then setting him on our bed in the master bedroom so I could get ready. I started to get dressed, putting on a brand new, light gray, single-breasted, three-button suit, a new French-cuffed white shirt, and silver and black striped tie in preparation for my meeting in downtown Minneapolis.

The new suit fit great and it felt good to be dressed up. Dressed and ready, I picked up Connor and carried him from the master bedroom into the Jeep, strapped him into his car seat with Snuffy, grabbed my briefcase, tossed it in the back of the Jeep, jumped in the front seat and turned on the engine. I looked down to find that Connor had already gone to the bathroom in his pull-up, and it had leaked out somehow—all over my brand new suit! I sat there stunned and kind of frozen. My new suit was probably ruined now, and there was no way I would make my meeting. I unhooked Connor from his car seat, carried him back into the house and started to cry. I was burning with frustration and anger at the same time, and I couldn't stop the tears. They kept coming like a river as I sat down on the hardwood floors of our living room, Indian style, holding Connor who was facing me, as he watched me cry.

I sat there on the floor, spent, looking up at our 26-foot ceilings in my brand new custom-made, soiled suit, holding Connor and sobbing. Connor was pawing my forehead as he sat on my legs saying *"Daddy cry. Daddy sad?"* He kept staring so peacefully as if he were trying to tell me that everything was going to be okay. It was as if he were trying to say, "Reach For Me" because everything was going to be okay. Like the peace was inside of him, so he was saying, "Daddy, just Reach For Me." I *wanted* the peace inside of him, with no fear, no cares in the world. Just total trust that Daddy knew what he was doing and was going to take care of him no matter the circumstance.

We sat there on the floor until I stopped crying, but I didn't want to get up. I just wanted to hold Connor. Right then, I *knew* I had to change, or I was going to come unglued. I had to change what I was doing to reduce the stress and anxiety, or I wouldn't be able to cope much longer. Things had been building up for so long, and I now realized that I had no control, wasn't going to be able to get back in control, and that perhaps I didn't **need** to be in control. It was a **radical** concept for me. It felt as though I had 500 pounds of bricks on my shoulders. Just then, the telephone rang. It was my father calling from Colorado.

"Hey there, Michael. What's up? How's your life going? Tell me what's up."

"Dad," I said, "This is not a good time to talk. I am sitting on the living room floor crying and holding Connor, and he just went to the bathroom all over my new suit, which is probably ruined now. I just can't do this anymore!"

"You can't do what anymore? I don't understand," he said.

"I can't do this anymore. I can't move. I am sad and I can't move. I don't know what to do anymore," I sobbed.

"What do you mean, you can't get up? What does that mean? Get up and get moving forward," he said.

"I just need to stay here with Connor for a minute and figure things out. I just need to think. I'll talk to you later." Then I hung up.

I was paralyzed from years of stress and anxiety building up with nowhere to go, and it all hit at once. Life was totally upside down. I'd moved from successful author of three business books, well-regarded keynote speaker, management consultant, and sales trainer to large and mid-sized corporations who thought our programs rocked—(they became required curriculum within several corporations)—to learning to be the father of a special-needs child, a child vulnerable and beautiful who needed me so much. I wanted whatever he had; his calm, his lack of worry and fear, and his sense of serenity. I wanted to feel all of these things as the stresses from over the years swirled in my head like some destructive tornado. We sat there on the hardwood floors of the living room, soiled suit and all, holding each other. And while Connor dried my eyes, I thought *I must figure things out*. Maybe I needed some help doing that.

This story stands out as perhaps the first time I began to acknowledge that I couldn't handle it by myself, that I was crumbling inside—and that I wasn't in control of my future, which was playing havoc on my mind, making me feel weak and unaccomplished. I was having trouble getting back on the horse of life; stuck in a thick quicksand.

Connor kept rubbing my arm and forehead as we got up off the floor. I took off my suit, changed him into a fresh pull-up, the second of the morning, cleaned him up and dropped him off a couple hours later at the morning care program. Since I'd rescheduled my meeting to another day, I went back to my home office and stared at my laptop motivated to do nothing. *What's going on? I'm in this massive trance and I can't get out of it.*

Being a man in charge and on-the-go was giving way to a deeper understanding of what it's like to feel like you are coming unglued—in your work life as you've known it, while your home life is just as stressful, but also sad and lonely. I'd had enough surprises for one lifetime, thank you very much. However, little was I to know there were more surprises ahead—things that would bring me to my knees and **force** some big changes. Stay with me, and I'll bring you inside these wonderful years.

You couldn't have choreographed a worse concatenation of events in a tighter span; learning of Connor's diagnosis between late fall of 2000 and the winter of 2001; attempting to digest the news and begin learning about Williams Syndrome, finding and then building relationships with doctors, therapists, treatments, and all; the shock of 9/11 and the devastation to people's spirits, beliefs and finances; the immediate spending freeze imposed by companies in several industry sectors, scaring employees and their families, and the overall manner in which the business community reacted—hunkering down and shutting off any/all perceived unnecessary expenditures. I was right there in the middle of it all with overwhelming fear, paralyzing sadness and uncertainty.

The services we'd been providing organizations didn't seem needed as companies slashed budgets on any training or consulting initiative unless it was mission critical to the business. Our programs were not viewed that way, regardless of how compelling my arguments that *this* was the time to invest. Deals got pushed into outer space. Multi-national clients with signed contracts began attempting to cancel, reduce their commitments, or not extend options, halting spending until the country could come up for air and deal with the aftermath from 9/11.

The stress was intense; explaining to investors why over $1 million in outstanding contracts was not coming in; sustaining a new bank line in place, and keeping the family income from going into the toilet. These things were all beyond my control, and it certainly felt like the man above was out to get me.

I reduced our family budget to less than we'd been used to, but enough to get through the drought until things started moving again. We were able to stay in our home, have two nice cars, plenty of food, money for our daughter's private basketball training and conditioning, business trips and vacations. Nothing was going into savings, but we'd make it through this temporary drought.

My wife appeared to understand the logic of why we needed to cut back while we and millions of other families rode out the ugly economic shock caused by 9/11, the tech sector tanking, the dot-com bust, and the fall-out from all of these shockwaves. Ask people in the investment-banking arena if they got lots of deals funded in this period of about three years, and see what they say. It was tough. But my family was getting what we needed. Thousands of companies had reportedly filed for bankruptcy, so I was aware of how tenuous things were. We'd figure out a way to make it through, God willing.

And though our marital relationship was cordial, respectful and focused on the children, there was no warmth, no snuggling, no intimacy—at least rarely. This is what I remember. Right or wrong, we had more important issues to deal with, so *"let's not push it"* was my thinking.

You can fault me all you want, thinking it was just plain dumb not to address the issues, but this appeared the wisest choice at the time. It's very easy to be an armchair quarterback, but I was picking my battles, and this one could wait until a better time. I couldn't let divorce be an option—no way, even though it had entered my mind from time to time. I considered it an irresponsible thing to do to my children. No way would I ever do that to my special-needs son, nor to my daughter. It seemed immature and selfish. Therefore, I would continue in an unhappy marriage because it was the most responsible thing to do for the family. That was my opinion at the time.

My wife, from what I could tell, was doing a good job holding down the fort when I traveled for client engagements, so it appeared her focus on the kids was as it should be. But what I couldn't see under the surface was that the stresses engulfing me were starting to show in her, though she was, in my opinion, better at disguising her feelings. In fact, so accomplished that, when the additional news hit, everyone, including me, was stunned. Just what I needed—another surprise!

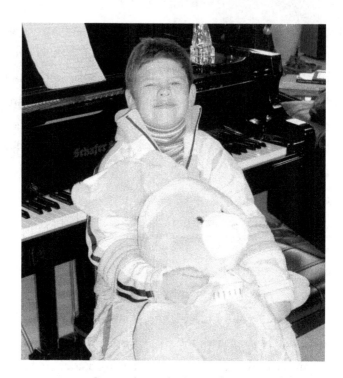

Connor loves the Easter Bunny

First Communion at St. Victoria Church

CHAPTER TEN

SURPRISE, SURPRISE! THE ICING ON THE CAKE (S)

I was in the office when I picked up the phone to my wife's shaken voice.

"Honey," she said, "I've been in a car accident. The kids and I are okay! Can you come right away?"

I flew out of the office, driving north on the main road to find the Navigator on the side of the road, my wife and kids inside, shaken but okay. Thank goodness for a heavy vehicle. According to my wife, a lady had pulled out in front of her, attempting to make a turn at the intersection. My wife professed that she had the right of way with a green light. The other party didn't see it that way, as I remember. Our insurance rates went up, the car was repaired, and life went on. The important thing was, no one was hurt.

Three or so months later, in the fall of 2003, while returning from a business trip, my cell phone rang. It was my wife. I was just getting off the plane.

"Our house has been broken into. Where are you?" she barked.

"During the day?" I asked. "I just landed. Are you okay? Where are the kids? What happened?"

"I'm okay," she said. "The kids are with me, standing here in the driveway. Police cars are here and the officers are inside checking everything out. Please get home as fast as you can!"

I flew down highway 494 watching for police the whole way, since I wasn't exactly driving the speed limit. When I arrived, I remember at least two squad cars in our driveway, and my wife shaking as I held her and the kids. I walked into the garage and in the back entryway to see music CDs thrown all over the living room floor. The stereo components were hanging from the shelves by their cables, yet nothing appeared to be stolen, just hanging by their respective power cords. How strange. They were after the sound system but didn't think to bring wire cutters?

The officer was dusting for fingerprints on the sound-system as another officer approached. He explained that, according to my wife, her wedding ring had been stolen along with her watch, some purses, earrings and a tennis bracelet, (if I recall properly). The officer told me to go into the master bedroom closet where I'd find another officer dusting for fingerprints. I followed his directions, to see my suits on the floor, yet none were missing. The officer was dusting the crystal ring box where we kept our wedding rings, which was chipped. I hadn't known my wife not to wear her wedding ring. But evidently she'd just gotten it back from the jeweler from either a cleaning and/or a repair. And for whatever reason, she wasn't wearing it on this day, and it was now evidently missing, if not stolen.

I walked all over the house inside and out with the officers, and from what I could tell, nothing seemed to be missing, except for her wedding ring, purses, earrings, and a tennis bracelet. This is what I remember. We went to the police station to be fingerprinted, and were told they searched the local pawnshops for the ring, but to no avail. I found her watch while searching in the back yard. It was sitting in a pile of grass clippings. She seemed surprised when I presented her with her watch. Her wedding ring never turned up. Insurance paid the claim on the stolen items, and she got a new ring, selecting the same setting I'd given her when I proposed, but a larger center stone. Case closed. With all the necessary focus on Connor and my daughter and all her activities, this was a distraction—another speed bump. As long as no one was hurt, we needed to put it behind us. I didn't spend two more minutes thinking about it!

I knew I was going to suffer a loss in the business that year, which I planned to cover by refinancing the house. So, later that fall of 2003, I met with a mortgage banker to inquire about refinancing our home mortgage.

"Yes, Mr. Boylan, plenty of equity in your house. That's a good thing—and a strong valuation on your appraisal, so this is also good. However, you have some credit issues, sir," the mortgage banker said with one eye on me, and the other on his computer screen.

"No, I don't think so," I said, confused as to what he was talking about.

"You do," he pressed. "You owe HFC thousands of dollars, which now appears delinquent."

"I don't have an account with HFC. This must be a mistake," I barked back.

"Yes, actually you do. It appears the account was opened a while back. And it looks as though you have at least one, maybe two other accounts with significant outstanding balances," he said, as if to scold me.

"This can't be correct," I said in disbelief.

"Well, from the looks of your credit report, you have some additional accounts, which are delinquent, then the one to HFC, all of which would need to be zeroed out if we refinanced your home. Because of the delinquencies, we won't be able to refinance under our standard products. We can still get it done. It'll just cost you a bit more, that's all."

Almost in disbelief, I asked, "How much do these delinquent accounts and credit cards total up to approximately?"

"You know," he said, "It's a significant number," turning the report around so I could see it, pointing to a number at the bottom of the page. "So again, as a condition of the refinance, we need to zero out these cards and accounts, then get the deal done for you. Sound good?" he said with a salesman's smile.

I left his office in a stupor. Was my wife hiding things from me? Why would she do that? We had a good life, a nice home, nice cars, nice clothes, she had a beautiful black full-length mink coat, we had our health, took great vacations, had plenty of food. Was there something more she needed? I couldn't imagine why she'd be hiding things, if she was. All the basics and more were covered. Yes, there was lots of stress related to the business challenges over the years related to the significant economic downturn of the dot.com bust and 9/11, which I was managing through. But she wouldn't hide things from me, would she?

I got in the Jeep, started for home, and called her, since she was home with the kids.

"Hi—are there some things I don't know about?" I said in an even-tempered tone.

From my memory, she seemed to know exactly what I was referring to, and said something to the effect of, "We can talk about it when you get home."

That night, after the kids were down, we sat on the kitchen floor, even tempered, with tears coming off and on. I listened to her explanation of why she had opened additional accounts and ran up balances, that she was sorry, and that it would *never* happen again. And that once I zeroed them out and we cut up the cards, keeping her on my American Express for emergencies, it would *never* happen again. We made peace, I accepted her apology, and trusted her word.

We got through Christmas of 2003 and went on a family ski trip to Colorado in the spring with some close friends and their kids—a much-needed getaway. We were able to leave Connor with a trusted part-time nanny we'd used over the years, who did a good job with him. It felt good to be in the Rocky Mountains for a week, having the chance to relax without Connor. As guilty as it felt to be away from him for just a week, it was important to have the short break.

When we got back, spring was beginning with my daughter's basketball season now done for the year, and AAU basketball firing up. Busy, busy, busy, go, go and go. Life was busy, and yet we had this beautiful little boy who needed us to go slower in many respects—to be calm, relaxed and peaceful. It was challenging to manage. We had a highly talented, accomplished, beautiful, athletic daughter, and a calm, cognitively challenged little boy who wanted to be held. Our children were incredibly different, requiring lots of emotional bandwidth from both of us.

As summer approached, we planned a family road trip to Colorado, where my father and his wife lived. While there, we'd visit friends over the fourth of July, a great time to be in Aspen. We'd stay in Snowmass where the kids could swim in the pool and we could all just relax.

Call me crazy, but I have good instincts from time to time. The ability to sense if something is not right, though I might not know exactly what. Anyway, I sensed my wife was being unusually cold and distant. Almost like she couldn't *stand* me anymore. Hence, the last few days of the trip were tense. Not many words were shared on the drive home as I remember across Highway 80 through Nebraska, then Iowa, and up Highway 35W to our home.

A few days after we got back, my wife and daughter flew to Atlanta for my daughter's AAU basketball tournament, while I stayed back to work and watch Connor. It was mid-summer 2004 and business was coming back again, thank God.

Question: You trust your spouse, don't you? Well I did. We were married. We took an oath on the altar before God, our family and lots of friends, to be faithful to one another in good times and in bad, 'til death do us part.' I think you've heard those lines a time or two.

I guess what's important in this part of the story, and why after conferring with mentors about including it, was that it could actually **help** other caregivers recognize that *receiving life-altering news* that your child is special-needs can transfer an intense amount of sadness, fear, anxiety and uncertainty onto the parents and related caregivers. You sometimes question how you're going to handle it all, while keeping your life moving forward as best you can.

The important thing here to ask, at least for me, is where does all that anxiety go? How does it get released? And in what form? And since **every single one of us** handles anxiety and stress in different ways, you can *never* be sure that those under the gun are coping just fine! How would you know for sure? Are you some psychic? I'm not. I knew I was stressed out, and was dealing with it as best I knew how. And from what I could tell, it seemed as though my wife was handling everything perhaps better than I was! How well do you really *know* your spouse? Now there's a question worthy of discussion. My point is; I'd had *enough* surprises over the last few years, with Connor's diagnosis being the biggest one of all. But like I said, there was more icing on the cake yet to come.

Hence, there was one more significant thing that happened that I learned about in July of 2004, which unfortunately, ended up being true. It was the icing on the cake that *forced* me to look up for answers, because I needed help comprehending it all. I will not share the nitty-gritty because it's too much; it's like a bad movie, and not necessary. And more importantly, because the real story is *not* about this terrible period, but rather, what I continue to learn from a cognitively challenged beautiful son named Connor. I can clearly remember upon learning of the news—my attorney saying something to the effect of, "Do you still want to stand beside her in this thing?" The specific allegations against my wife (now ex-wife), I will not reveal. I love my daughter, so it does not need to be shared. She loves her mother very much, and it could damage my relationship with my daughter if I shared the details—though they are true. Therefore, I will not. Its called taking the high road. And for those who feel this is simply not fair—I apologize. My relationship with my daughter is more important. Secondly, the media is **much** about focusing on controversy. If they can't find a controversy, they'll create one, since it helps drive the ratings, which is what it's all about for network media. And though there was plenty of unbelievable controversy during this period, this book is not about this family tragedy, which it was; but about what I continue to learn on my journey as a caregiver of a special-needs child.

Suffice it to say that we are now divorced. And it's in the past, thanks to counseling sessions over the years and friends who are Catholic priests willing to provide guidance. Thank God for time to heal, reflect, and look for a deeper understanding. And to forgive, which I have done.

My plea for caregivers of special-needs children and all those who are friends and extended family is to be **aware** of the **significant stresses** and **pressures** caregivers are under from time to time—which are nearly **impossible** to escape. And let's be clear—they are often forever! It is this level of stress and anxiety that can, in some cases, cause people to do things that are not good for them, their families or society. The **critical lesson** for us all is to be aware, and helpful to anyone who is a caregiver of a special-needs child. You may genuinely help them through a challenging time, allowing them to help themselves, their family, their special-needs children and our society.

For the sake of our memories, and because we can all be unbelievably quick to point the finger pretty harshly at others about this or that—let's remember why I choose to share a small portion of this part of the story. First, because it's true as best I can remember. Second is not to discredit my ex-wife, though her actions hurt me, and our family. The story is what it is, and it happened. My intent is to bring **awareness** to the **amount** of stress, strain and uncertainty on the caregivers of special-needs children, which is very real! And to help people recognize that sometimes, this constant gnawing can cause people to do things that cause damage to themselves, their families, and their special-needs children.

This is precisely why we need to be aware of the stress and strain on a good number of the estimated 35 million caregivers of special-needs children in the U.S. alone. And why it's a good idea to make sure caregivers get some help, so they can continue to care for themselves and their special-needs children.

Was it this level of stress and anxiety that caused my ex-wife to act out? No one knows. But these things were the culmination of events that caused our marriage and family to come apart as a result, and *that* is the tragedy here. It has impacted our family and our children.

If you are asking yourself what should you do in the event that you and your family are going through extremely challenging times right now to avoid or better navigate through what might be happening in your family or in your marriage, that is a good question. And one that would garner 100 different responses from 100 different marriage and family therapists. But my answer as someone who has lived through this prolonged desert and fire experience and has come out the other side, is to offer suggestions that I hope are helpful to you, your spouse or significant other, and other members of your family. And I hope you take them to heart, because there is *nothing* to joke around about when it comes to dealing with heightened and prolonged levels of stress, anxiety, worry, doubt, or depression, and how they can negatively impact your own personality, the relationship with your spouse or significant other, and other members of your family.

Hindsight being what it is, I am sure that I could have and should have done a better job of addressing the stress that was going on within me, and my wife. And being honest about it. I take responsibility for that. In my case, a type "A" personality of "we are going to hunker down and power through this thing" was probably stupid, not to mention unhelpful to me and my family. Being stubborn and bull-headed (men especially) is not smart when you are in the eye of the storm, don't have *all* the answers, and probably should be reaching out to others for help to make it through. I did not do this, and *that* was a big mistake. Men often have the instinct of wanting to "fix" things, without asking for help. Again, a dumb move when you have a special-needs child. How do you "fix" a special-needs diagnosis in a child? You often can't. But you **must** figure out how to accept it, learn to live with it, and somehow become grateful for the new life it will bring you and your family.

Caregivers of children with special-needs don't get much relief, are often exhausted as I was, and often isolate themselves when under intense duress because they often do not know where to turn for help. Or they feel as if no one can help them anyway, so it's up to them to power through on their own. Again, dumb thinking. It is no surprise that the divorce rate among caregivers of children with special-needs is through the roof. It is unbelievable how prolonged periods of stress can essentially destroy any feelings or desire for romance in a relationship, turning those thoughts into a thing of the past, where you wonder where those feelings went. Caregiving can take an immensely harmful toll on any marriage or special relationship. It also impacts the dynamic of parenting with your other children if you have more than one. And it impacts the family dynamic itself. I am not embellishing. So how do you protect yourself, your relationship, and your family in situations of intense challenge to ensure that you will make it through and survive? Is there some checklist or **road map** to follow to help you make it through? My answer is, yes. It is coming in later chapters, and it's called *The Connor Principles*, a *step-by-step process* designed to help you address key issues that in your eyes, are going on in your marriage or significant relationship and in the family, to reduce stress, anxiety, avoid depression hopefully, and help you and your family make it through. Perhaps even empower you with a renewed outlook and sense of purpose. A tall order indeed, and there are no guarantees that it will give you all of these things. However, as one who has lived through a tremendously difficult period of several years and is still walking around—this *step-by-step process* can help you better manage and make it through. This is my hope.

The icing on the cake(s) had come, and they were not sweet. The surprises were not happy ones. But as some people say, sometimes from the darkest and most challenging period in your life—which for me was a period of years—can come a genuine turning point! A true change in your life's compass heading. And though it often felt as though I had no compass heading during this period and was treading in a bottomless ocean of choppy water, **this was the series of events that forced** me to look up for help. I needed some peace as all four tires were flat and I didn't see any stations on the side of the road where I could pull over and fill them up. No more surprises! Please. No more surprises.

WHAT'S THE PICTURE LOOKING FORWARD?

I don't know how you are, but if I can't see the picture forward, I can't function very well. It's what keeps me going, in a sense. And there was no picture now. Instead, I was sitting on the edge of a cliff looking out over the expanse of water, on the phone with my mother asking for the phone number of my aunt, a Carmelite Nun of 45-plus years. She was one of the wisest people I knew, and the person who called my mother the morning of my car accident, saying something to the effect that my face had appeared to her in a dream, that she'd been called to pray for me and wanted to know if I was all right. This was hours before my mom got the call from the hospital in Billings, Montana that I'd been in a serious car accident and had broken my back pretty badly. Ever since then, I felt my aunt was *wired* directly to The Man Upstairs, and I wanted to talk to her. I had had it! I was tired of it all! *What was happening to me and my life?*

I had no idea what the future looked like for me. It felt like I was in a knock-down, drag-out battle with God over exactly who had control over my life! I was out of steam, with hardly the energy to look for the positive, since it felt as though I'd been dealt the harshest deck of cards on the poker table of life. There were therapist meetings, doctors appointments, clinical evaluations and assessments, heart checkups, his Individualized Educational Plan (IEP is the lingo for caregivers), helping coordinate the team of teachers, therapists, the paraprofessional, and the outside therapists not connected to the school district but through my private insurance, so we were all on the same page in terms of working toward a common set of goals for Connor.

The IEP was the guidepost we were all attempting to follow to help Connor make progress. My ex-wife and I would meet with four to eight people every six months to assess progress, discuss areas of concern, and make refinements to the IEP as new behaviors emerged. And all handled as if nothing ever happened between my ex-wife and me—civil and diplomatic. Tell me *that* didn't require some energy! It was all for Connor's growth and development. On top of this, I had to work! I still needed an income to pay the bills and child support. (Yes, I had to pay child support, though Connor was with me about 50 percent of the time and my daughter, unfortunately, was living with her mother.) I didn't understand how single fathers involved with their children's schooling, teachers meetings, activities and all kept up the pace. This continues to be a commitment on top of all the care, therapy sessions, corresponding reports and paperwork associated with getting Connor what he needs. It's not an option to do it any other way.

Because of my personality, I always needed to see the picture looking forward to visualize where I was headed. The picture of myself had changed from Joe Business Boy to soon-to-be full-time caregiver of a special-needs child. It was such a radical change in my self-picture that everything was up for grabs now. The image I had of myself, and what I thought was important, had all blown up. I felt like an unattractive, unwanted, under-accomplished entrepreneur of 20-plus years, struggling author, management consultant and sales trainer on thin ice, needing to remold my work around Connor, while providing everything he needed. Personally, I didn't think I could do it. I needed to redesign myself into a more calm, relaxed, less type-A, peaceful and present father of huge emotional bandwidth for a son so very sensitive, gentle and tender, so I could be available to him whenever he needed.

It would take time to build this new person. Especially because of how I was raised; the first-born son of a major-league taskmaster for whom accomplishing the task at hand, then moving on to the next one, was key! It's what life was all about—getting things done! But it seemed that now, that wasn't important anymore. Instead, it was about being *present* for Connor. It sounds so simple and basic, yet it is very hard to do.

Becoming a calmer, more relaxed, less paced person is what Connor needed. But in reality, it was also what I needed or I'd blow up! The old me would need to go away now—be put in a box and laid to rest. A new me would need to be born, tailored to what he needed: a gentler, slower-paced, relaxed life. How I'd go about this transformation I had no idea, but I knew it was paramount, or we'd both go in the tank! I had no other option. I'd have to change my work life. I'd have to manage therapists, paraprofessionals and other caregivers, most of which were women, in our case. I'd have to create a super-organized system to keep up with the volume of correspondence and paperwork, which was intense. There was and is often daily correspondence between his teachers, the paraprofessional and therapists, since without a full-time paraprofessional Connor could easily disrupt the flow for the other 25 or so children in the classroom. The picture was definitely going to have to change to satisfy Connor's growth process in all areas.

The hardest thing for me in all of this was feeling as though I was in a constant wrestling match with God, and that at every turn, I was being pinned down on the wrestling mat of life. Forced to listen and ask for guidance. The feeling was this strong! I kept asking for some PEACE—GOD DAMN IT! That would be nice! How about just a smidgeon of peace and calm?

Each day, I put on soft music around 7 a.m., the time Connor typically started to wake up, regardless if he was in my bed or his own bed across the hall. Yanni, Enya, soft piano music, Andrea Bocelli—any music that helped him wake up to a gentle environment, helped him throughout his day. This became part of our daily routine when he was with me, as the schedule became one week with me, then one week with his mother, and so on. It was this way for a few years after the divorce, and then it changed. I became the full-time caregiver when my ex-wife decided to move to the East Coast permanently.

Everything was and still is about *structure* and *routine* for Connor. He needs it to function. Creating and showing him a picture schedule of the four to five activities in a row we'd need to complete, as part of our morning routine seemed to help his mind process what came next. The order of things was and still is very important, and if I changed the order in any way, it was a real problem from Connor. We stuck to a routine when he was with me. I'd make his lunch before he got up, write in his daily diary that went back and forth between the paraprofessional, his mother and me so we could keep in communication about how each day went; take off his soaked pull-up, put on a fresh one, brush his teeth, let him relax and chat with Snuffy (his purple blanket), talk to *the bug* (another imaginary friend) and play piano in the living room. Then we'd go downstairs so Connor could *pound* on the drums (which helped his entire system to fire), then breakfast, shower, hair dried, lotion on, get dressed, and off to school at 9:10. I'd visit with the paraprofessional about how the morning went, which would definitely impact how his day went at school. Connor had therapy after school two days a week, which was in addition to the therapy services he received during school from additional professionals. It all became routine fast because it had to. Connor had to have routine. His brain had to have it. Any other way caused too much strife for him.

I'd restructured things so my new window to work was essentially 9:45 a.m. to 3:30 p.m. during the weeks I had Connor. I'd pick him up from school at 3:45 p.m. then we'd go to therapy from 4 p.m. to 5 p.m. two days a week. When there wasn't soccer, we'd go straight home to play, and then have dinner. I'd read to him, or snuggle in front of the fireplace with his blanky, which helped him wind down before bedtime, around 8:30 p.m. If I wasn't wiped out by the time he went down, I'd work until I was too tired.

This became my new life, focused on and around him. I never thought I'd need to become a full-time mom and dad, but that's exactly what was happening. I became a 360-degree parent of a beautiful and cognitively challenged first-born son.

One particular morning, Connor had a cold, so I let him sleep until after 8 a.m., causing a bit of a rush in our morning routine. He awoke to calm music, chatted with Snuffy, I got him fed, brushed his teeth, wiped his mouth thoroughly so no toothpaste residue was on his face (which caused him to fixate on whatever it was that was still on his face), then led him into the shower. I held his hand firmly, since his overall balance isn't the best. (It must have something to do with his vestibular system, because if he's not totally centered, he might easily just wipe out. He sometimes operates by bumping into things, then re-tacking after he hits something; a wall, a pole, people, etc.)

Anyway, we were in a bit of a rush on this particular day—my fault for not adjusting to him. I got him into the shower with me, turned around for just *two seconds* to grab the shampoo to wash his hair, and WHAM! He wiped out, hitting his head on the glass wall of the shower. So there I was—holding my child on the floor of the shower at 8:45 in the morning, while most people have already been at work for an hour or so, water pouring down on both of us, as my son sobbed, and sobbed, and sobbed, me rubbing his forehead as I held him, trying to calm him down.

All I could think was—THIS IS MY LIFE NOW! This has *got* to be a test—*and a test I will not fail! It's just such a radical shift,* I kept thinking.

I used to get up early, work out and get to the office by 7:30 a.m. to begin the day. Now I'm giving my son a shower at 8:45 a.m. as he cries and cries, repeating to me over and over again, *"I bonked it,"* as he points to his head.

It was as if I were outside myself looking down on Connor and me on the floor of the shower thinking, *"Okay, it's going to be okay. Just calm down ... c-a-l-m down."*

As I lifted Connor from the floor of the shower and grabbed a towel to dry his eyes, he looked up at me, smiled, pressed his face right up against mine and said in the happiest voice, "I know you! You're a nice boy! Aw, Daddy. You're a nice boy!"

Wow! Just another one of the many *immediate* shifts in moods throughout the day, this one delightful, almost like an angelic reminder of how special this child is to me. I never knew when the swings were coming, but it didn't matter, since they are frequent. It was part of the foundation for becoming a calmer person, so I could better handle the swings and be present instead of all stressed out when they came on.

The picture looking forward was way too fuzzy, almost like there was some kind of writer's strike, and the scripts for the coming series hadn't been written yet.

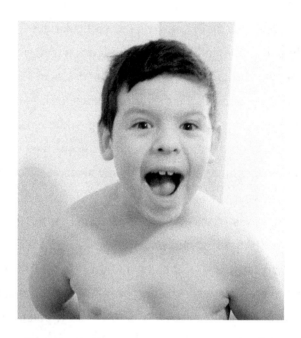

Chapter Twelve

HAVE SOME FAITH, MAN!
YOU'RE NEVER GIVEN MORE THAN YOU CAN HANDLE

Whoever said this has *never* lived through difficult times! At least, that's what I thought. I'd *never* had the wind taken out of my sails like this before. I thought eventually the winds of my own internal motivation would pick up as they always had before, and I'd be sailing along again in no time. That had always been the case before with other challenges I'd encountered in sports, life and business. But that didn't happen this time. In fact, I went in the opposite direction on some *path* for a deeper set of answers, as I constantly threw out questions about what this was all about—and why? Why was *He* after *me?*

"What do you want?" I would yell, when no one could hear me. If I asked 10 times, I asked it a hundred times a week. So much had happened in rapid succession that it truly felt as though someone was trying to speak to me, deliberately slow me down and get my attention by grinding me to a halt. I didn't know if my own internal winds would ever pick up again. I'd been halted for some reason, and I started looking up for the first time in my life for answers, but through a deep anger and resentment, because I was sure I was being singled out, picked on and given undue levels of stress that I had no capability of handling.

It felt defeating that everyone around me seemed to be sailing along with a strong wind at his or her back. They had a gentle glide path up and forward, with life being relatively free of obstacles, but not for me. Every time I attempted to get back on the horse in the business I'd been in for 12-plus years, bigger speed bumps appeared. It literally felt as though someone was sending a message that something different was ahead. But still no pictures of what *that* was. It was maddening. I had to make a living, and the stress of reshaping the business around Connor and the care he needed was, and still is, challenging.

Was I being buffed for something else? It would be nice if I had a clue about what *that* might be. I wanted to be left alone so I could get back on the horse, and ride into a successful life. Problem was, my whole picture of success was in flux.

"Are you okay? Is everything all right? You just seem so different now. You're so quiet these days. Don't you want to join us for dinner?"

This was a typical comment from friends during this dark and lonely period of adjusting to my new personality. I just preferred to be alone with Connor. And during the off weeks when he wasn't with me, I kept to myself. I missed both my children, and having an empty house was depressing. Perhaps I was becoming an introvert. Who knows? I just wanted some peace, some grace. I was searching for answers. The concept of faith had always made sense, but I'd been beaten down so thoroughly that I didn't see the real benefit anymore. Faith? For what? It certainly hadn't played out very well for me so far.

Have some faith, Man? I needed to find some—and fast. Was anyone going to turn on the lights in the near future so I could find my bearings, and figure out how to move forward again? That would sure be nice.

WHO'S DRIVING THIS BUS? I DIDN'T SIGN UP FOR THIS!

W ho doesn't like control? Kind of a dumb question since we all know that having a handle on the direction you're headed is a good thing, and a necessity of sorts. Problem is, you need to be driving the bus to control its destiny, and I wasn't driving anymore. I'd been tossed out of the driver's seat and told to sit in the back for a while. To be more honest, I'd given up wrestling for control of the wheel since I was at my wits' end and was convinced someone didn't want me driving; instead, I was to chill out for a while and be patient! How nice! *Be patient for what?* I kept asking.

If you're not in the driver's seat of life, we all know you will surely end up in one of a hundred places; exactly what I was worried about. Like we talked about, control wasn't mine. Determination? Internal motivation? They'd all passed me by, though I hadn't signed up for any of it. I was a driver by nature, but the wheel had been given to someone else now. The old tapes in my mind since I was a boy—about making sure I was firmly in charge of my family's destiny—were all being challenged to their core now.

Self-doubt is a killer drug and I'd overdosed on it for the last several years. Worry and fear was all over my face. I couldn't get rid of it. A perfect combination for trying to convince new client's to come aboard.

One spring Thursday, I picked up Connor from his Montessori school at the usual time, 3:45 p.m. On this particular day he came at me in a beeline yelling, *"Daddy! Daddy!"* falling into my arms in a full-on collapse. He'd had it *locked* into his mind since morning that when we got home, Joe, the lawnmower man, and his crew, would be at our house to mow the yard. This was the highest of high points for Connor; watching Joe, Jason and Matt—the lawnmower guys, as they mowed, trimmed and weed-whacked their way around our yard for a good couple of hours. Connor would sit on our front stoop, totally mesmerized, rocking back and forth, watching ever so loyally as they made their way around the yard. Hog heaven for Connor! *Nothing* beat this! He was in over-drive when they were at the house every week. And when they weren't, he talked about Joe ALL THE TIME! Something about Joe, combined with the sounds the mowers and whackers made, was music to Connor's ears, though he'd cover them with his hands or wear his sound-deadening headphones to lessen the intensity of the noise.

On this beautiful afternoon, we sat together on the front stoop, waiting for Joe and his crew to arrive. Connor asked about *every 180 seconds* if Joe was coming. With every car that passed, Connor would stand and yell, "Joe is coming. I know Joe is coming. Oh, there's Joe. Here he comes!"

I needed to be calm in these times because he was beside himself with anticipation, rocking back and forth, fists opening and closing as fast as he could go. Being calm in these times took *lots* of energy and patience.

Around 6 p.m. after being asked 50-plus times if Joe was coming (and responding as if I'd never heard the question—calm and gentle), the phone rang. It was Joe. His mowers had broken down and he wasn't coming today; maybe tomorrow, if he could get them fixed. Connor, unable to comprehend or process why he wasn't coming, just that he wasn't, went into an uncontrollable sob—a lonesome cry that overtook him, moving him from high-as-a-kite elation moments earlier, to utter sadness all in a few moments. *Stay calm*, I kept saying to myself. I held him as he sobbed and rocked back and forth. Then, after about 10 minutes, he stopped, pressed his nose against mine and said, "Tomorrow? Joe is coming tomorrow?"

I couldn't answer with a hopeful response because he'd immediately *lock on* and begin the fixations on the next day, which of course would end in disaster if Joe didn't show up. I tried not to mention Joe until I knew he was within earshot. That lessened the angst.

"We'll see, Honey, we'll see," I said, as I rubbed the tears from his innocent face. I wasn't up for another day of this so I couldn't tell him. Fixations were, and still are, *huge* for Connor and there are many different kinds; trains, mowers and blowers, the car wash, candy, saxophones and violins, loud noises (which can set him off), the mail and the post office, and many more. And newer fixations appeared often, like later that night, after I'd gotten him wound down and was feeding him some dinner.

I tore off a paper towel, put it under the faucet, put some soap on it, and began wiping off the kitchen counter as I'd done a *thousand times* before, in front of him. But not this time. He started yelling to stop, kicking the kitchen cabinets with his feet, covering his ears profusely.

"What, Honey? What?" I said trying to understand what was wrong.

"Stop that noise," he barked, as he began crying again. "Hurts my ears."

This sent Connor back into a high-anxiety state, adding to the wind-down time.

Later that night, after playing music and reading to him, it was time for bed. We went through our routine: brushing his teeth, then potty, then jammies, prayers, etc. However, oftentimes, Connor's brain doesn't tell him when he needs to go to the bathroom, and sometimes there's a mad dash to the toilet. Even after we've gone 20 or so minutes earlier. It can happen in the car, on the soccer field, in the grocery store, in a gondola in Colorado, anywhere. Sometimes we make it in time, sometimes we don't. I'd just taken him potty 30 minutes earlier, so I thought we were in good shape.

"Hurry, hurry, hurry," he started chanting. I knew what that meant. We spun around to the toilet, quickly helping him pull down his jammies and pull-up, but not in time. Connor let it fly with fire-hose intensity all over my hand! Standing there, with my hand dripping wet with urine running down onto the floor, I thought, *This is hard!*

This was the second time today he had urinated on my hand because we didn't make it in time. (We usually have about 30 seconds after Connor tells me.)

Remain calm, I kept telling myself; *It's not his fault. He can't help it, and he's not doing it on purpose. This is not about you! It's about taking care of him, so just chill out.* I kept repeating in my mind.

I never know when things are going to hit, so it's challenging to remain centered and not on edge, since this became another normal day for Connor and me.

I got us cleaned up, put another pull-up on him and we were finally ready for bed. Since the divorce, I'd had the toughest time keeping him in his own bed. I don't know why, nor could he tell me, other than he was scared. Separation anxiety? Don't know, but I wasn't going to give him the third degree. If he wanted to sleep in my bed, then fine.

I got him all tucked in with Snuffy, made the sign of the cross on his forehead, said our prayers, climbed in, read him a story and then turned out the light.

Around 2 a.m. Connor awoke and sat straight up like a steel pole, scaring the hell out of me. He started rocking back and forth, covering his ears because he could hear a train (miles from our house) and it hurt his ears.

"Daddy, what color's train? It hurts me. What color is … red?"

"I don't know, Honey, I don't know, Connor. Daddy hold your ears until the train goes night-night, okay?"

Sometimes the train horn, as he called it, would go on and on. I'd hold him as he rocked in tears because the noise hurt. More tears again at about 4 a.m. when he heard another one from a dead sleep. Not a good night. I was exhausted. Up at 6:30 a.m., Connor took Snuffy and went into the laundry room, patiently peering out over the washer into our front yard. *"Joe is coming? I know he's here."* I wasn't ready to deal with the Joe issue just yet. Another day had begun and we'd do it all over again.

Expectations can be good and bad, sometimes harmful to your mental health. They can cause huge levels of stress, anxiety and anger when the things *you* want, expect or have been planning on happening just aren't or never will. I was coming to grips with the fact that this new life of mine was the way it was going to be for as far forward as I dared look. I didn't expect any of this and wasn't that happy about it either, to be frank. I kept thinking about how my life used to be, orderly, planned, fun and structured. However, I was learning to be an ever-calm, sensitive caregiver, relying on vast amounts of emotional patience to help my mentally challenged *Angel Child*—a child that needed me more than I ever expected, perhaps for as long as I am alive. I didn't expect that one! I thought my son would grow up playing sports of all kinds like his dad, have tons of friends and a relatively easy childhood, go to college, get married and maybe have children someday. You know, the typical American dream; the *normal* track that it seems so many people follow. But maybe most of these things would never come true now. Should I wallow in self-pity because I'd been cheated out of having a child with a more *normal* upbringing? Or learn to reshape my own expectations into a new set that were being molded day by day? I knew the right answer.

True, I didn't sign up for any of this, but does anyone sign up for his or her life? It just felt like the one picked for me was something well beyond my capability to cope with and manage. But there was no other choice; so learning to change into a new person was the way it was going to have to be. End of story. A 360-degree father (and mother, since I was now single and had no help when he was with me) was the bus trip I was on now. I wasn't driving the bus anymore, and needed to get comfortable with that fact, or it would drive me crazy! Control Boy needed to chill out and find a new level of peace in being gentle, present and calm for my son. No other options made sense.

1) If mega challenges, such as raising a special-needs child, can teach us such powerful lessons about the simplicity and depth of life, how are you doing in this area of **control**, as either a relatively new caregiver of a special-needs child, or a veteran who's been at it for a while?

2) Did you go through a phase where you felt as though you where in a battle for **control** of your own life?

3) How is it turning out so far? What are you learning, and what's "the new normal" for you?

4) What things are you struggling with in your role as a caregiver of a special-needs child?

Independence Pass

Connor's imaginary friend, the "bug"

First day at music and dance camp—Challenge Aspen

CHAPTER FOURTEEN

WHAT AM I, YOUR SERVANT?

How do you act when you've been pushed to the wall by your kids or whomever, and you feel as though your life is no longer your own, but in fact like you work for them? And you feel like barking, **"What am I, your servant?"** This is exactly how I felt, wondering if there was anyone else in the country whose life had been upended like mine, and **forced** to reorganize everything in order to focus on my special-needs child. My work life, business relationships, friendships, personality, you name it—it all had to change in some fashion to accommodate what Connor needed.

Lying in bed one night during a week when Connor was with his mother, I was doing a marvelous job of feeling sorry for myself. My whole life seemed to revolve around Connor—from the time he awoke to the time he went down. There were also follow-up emails to therapists, his paraprofessional and teachers, adjustments to his IEP, frequent assessments of his progress, tweaking of his occupational and physical therapy plans and sessions, doctors appointments, etc. Oh—and work stuff too! Somewhere in there I had to work.

The night was quiet, a rare moment to myself. I reached over and grabbed *The Purpose Driven Life* by Rick Warren, a recent purchase based on the recommendation of a few friends. Maybe I'd find some comfort from the thing. The book fell onto my stomach opening to the beginning of chapter 25 entitled, "Transformed By Trouble." How weird was that—especially since my life seemed like it had become one massive series of troubles leading to the next?

I began reading, yellow highlighter in hand, when I was drawn like a laser beam to the following passage:

"God uses problems to draw you closer to himself. The Bible says, The Lord is close to the brokenhearted; he rescues those who are crushed in spirit."

THAT WAS ME! I was brokenhearted. Is *that* what he was doing? Drawing me closer to him? What for? Things always needed to line up for me. The paragraph went on:

"Your most profound and intimate experiences of worship will likely be in your darkest days—when your heart is broken, when you feel abandoned, when you're out of options, when the pain is great—and you turn to God alone. It is during suffering that we learn to pray our most authentic, heartfelt, honest-to-God prayers. Problems force us to look to God and depend on him instead of ourselves. You'll never know that God is all you need until God is all you've got!"

This phrase hit me like a lightning bolt. I read on as if He was speaking directly to me. Maybe He was.

"There's a Grand Designer behind everything. Your life is not a result of random chance, fate, or luck. There is a master plan. God is pulling the strings. God's plan for your life involves all that happens to you—including your mistakes, your sins, and your hurts. Under pressure, your faith-life is forced into the open and shows its true colors."

I lay there rereading these phrases, soaking them in. It *did* feel like He was speaking directly to me, and it felt safe. *Was this all part of some grand design? If so, what for, and what's the design?* I asked. I'd LOVE to know. Then I read one more phrase:

"If a jeweler's hammer isn't strong enough to chip off our rough edges, God will use a sledgehammer. If we're really stubborn (me in spades) *he uses a **jackhammer**. He will use whatever it takes."*

This phrase stopped me cold. This was happening to me! He was using a jackhammer on me to get my attention! Holy buckets! This is real. So why does He want my attention? For what? Was Connor being born to me, and were all the crazy and horrible things that had happened all part of the Grand Design to push me over the edge? Why? What did He want from me, or what did He want me doing, for that matter? Actually, I wanted to be left alone, since it felt as though I was being badgered, picked on, pushed to the limit, and singled out. It was amazingly strange. It felt like I was being hunted and couldn't get away. And trust me—I was trying. Trying to bring my own plan of attack back from the dead, but every time I did, new obstacles were thrown in my path. What in the world was happening? What's the big secret? I'd really love to know, damn it!

These questions came out in machine-gun fashion, though the answers didn't come overnight. They unfolded over the coming years as various signs came through unusually coincidental events; the timing of them and their significance began to create a road map to a place I couldn't quite see yet. But clearly, a path was being carved out with me trying to make heads or tails out of which way to follow.

It did feel as though I was being whittled down to nothing. My confidence was in the toilet, not an attractive quality. My self-esteem was nonexistent. My former upbeat outlook on life was nowhere to be found. Why? What a total waste. This can't be what I was called to do—be a sourpuss.

I kept on reading about surrender and surrendering; surrendering unto HIM and asking for direction and guidance. I thought I'd been doing that over the years, but evidently, not enough! **And if you think this all made total sense to me—you are nuts!** It was so confusing; since this was the total *opposite* of everything I'd been taught about how to get ahead in life! I was taught that those who took the bull by the horns and pressed forward, those were the people who got ahead in life. Those were the folks who made things happen— made something of themselves and succeeded in life. You didn't accomplish great things by surrendering! Impossible! I mean, for crying out loud, no way could you get anything of significance done by surrendering; by being a wall-flower—meek, congenial and blowing in the wind. Who succeeds with this type of bent on life? Show me **one person** and maybe I'd consider taking on a new angle around this thing called surrender. No way can you accomplish anything by surrendering! Though there was this one guy named Jesus who actually did accomplish quite a bit in the world through surrender.

After months of pondering the concept of surrender and what it meant to me, the weirdest things started happening. I started to gain more perspective, become calmer and not so wound like a top. A level of peace came into me that I'd never experienced before. The surrender concept started to find a home in me as I began to ask for more direction and peace, more frequently than I'd ever done before. It felt good actually, and still does. It seemed to help prevent me from getting wound up about this or that. It's not magical, but it helped keep me from fixating on how things were all going to come together. Was this some transformation I was going through? I can't say, because I don't really know. But I was learning to serve Connor and all of his needs, and as life went on, I gained more serenity from surrendering from life as I once knew it—fast-paced with all the goings-on, traveling throughout the country and internationally, meeting influential people—to a simple existence around my new life of caregiver to my son.

True, I didn't have a choice. But my former lifestyle could have sent me to my grave sooner than later if I didn't learn a new pattern of life around my son. Forced to learn it? Sure, you could say that. But I started to feel that through surrender, I would learn a new depth to life that I'd never experienced before.

"What am I, your servant?" In one sense, I was learning the answer was yes, and feeling empowered by it. Maybe even lucky that I'd been given a cognitively challenged son who was teaching me more about life than any teacher I'd ever had. Was I lucky to have a special-needs child with all that meant over a lifetime? Yes, was my answer, and I found that answer through surrender.

QUESTIONS TO CONSIDER:

1) What has the concept of surrender taught you? Or haven't you surrendered anything yet?

2) How do you make it real in your own life on your journey as a care-giver of a special-needs child?

3) Is there *anything* in your daily routine you could change or eliminate that might bring more "calm" into your own path?

WHAT WILL I LEARN AND WHAT AM I SUPPOSED TO DO WITH IT?

Here's another fabulously creative approach to allowing **control** to enter right back into my life, after I was doing a pretty cool job with this new concept of surrender.

As clients, associates and colleagues began learning that I had a special-needs child, some would say things like, "Wow, that's got to be tough, I mean really *tough*. I just can't imagine. But at the end of the day, what have you *learned* from it?"

It's funny how we're all programmed in one way or another, around **business** and the need to quantify how each *situation* is to be learned from, extracted from and then applied. At least men seem to be this way for the most part, always needing to quantify **the experience** so they can keep score. Maybe women are this way as well. I can't say because I don't know. As if we're all trying to climb that ever-invisible ladder to the sky with a better job, better houses and more expensive cars, fancier clothes and trips, bigger lives, and cooler friends, as we rise above the fray to hang with the big hitters. It's like some academic exercise designed to help quantify **the experience** so that it can help us get to *that next level*. It's also sad to learn how wired we are to the concept of climbing to "that next level." God forbid we go backwards in life, like I'd been doing—in my opinion—for the past several years. I had nothing to show for it in terms of financial gain—usually how most of us measure whether we're moving forward or not.

But I *did* start asking myself these very same questions. What was I going to do with this new, gentler personality I was taking on? What financial benefits, if any, would it bring? And what was I going to do with the new skill sets I was learning around how to care for Connor, in a world where the woman traditionally has been more of the nurturer, the caregiver, the one who was always there? I don't know if the stereotype has much relevance anymore in our times, but I was sure learning a lot—some of it painful and massively time-intensive. But maybe it would end up being of value to someone someday.

One thing I have learned since taking on more of an introvert's personality so I can be patient and calm for Connor—and more observant—is how incredibly self-consumed and self-impressed many of us are from one day to the next. And how harsh we often are about other people's life interruptions—as if they did something to *deserve* their misfortune and lifelong stresses. And how most of us are exceptionally talented at inventing impressive-sounding rationales as to why it's really not our "gig" to understand the stresses or the strains on parents and related caregivers of special-needs children—the **35 million** or so **caregivers** just in the United States—because, as many people so eloquently put it, *"This might sound really bad, or cold and callous and harsh, but at the end of the day, I'm sorry, but I don't see how this whole thing, as horrible as it is for some people, and I wouldn't want to change places with them for all the tea in China—but I don't see how it impacts me per se. I'm just saying. Do you know what I mean?"*

To that attitude, I say what a **cop-out** and a **total shame**, because this issue does indeed impact every single **employer organization**, citizens, (meaning all of us, unless you're not a taxpayer), our educational system, the medical establishment, families and the **state** and **federal government** to the tune of **billions** and **billions** of dollars each and every year!

However, I'm a big boy who understands that it often takes a major life jolt or trauma to cause most of us to wake up, pay attention, and look at things from outside of ourselves, and through a different lens. And though it's hard to admit but very true, it usually needs to impact people in their **pocketbooks** in a negative, significant fashion, and then magically, you've got their attention! As the political pollsters like to say, *"It's the economy, Stupid!"* More often than not, it usually needs to be about the money, before most of us pay close attention. This is not me being negative, but rather, mature, as this is what I have learned the hard way. The scope of this issue, with millions of parents and related caregivers caring for special-needs children, equates to billions of dollars at issue. And billions of the caregivers' **own money** put forth for extra levels of care and attention needed for their children. This is why you might think twice about reaching out to your neighbors down the street, your co-workers, fellow parishioners within your church, people you encounter at the grocery store or mall, etc., who are caregivers. You'd be shocked how far a kind gesture toward them, like a smile, kind word, or yes—even a few dollars thrown their way, might provide some relief for those dealing with their lot in life, though few of us, if any, are looking for a hand-out. We are not. But the once-in-a-blue-moon surprise gesture from a **non-caregiver** goes a long way to help—with you and/or the non-caregiver benefiting just as much as the recipient of your kindness. Something to ponder.

As my life has been jolted, I have taken on a different lens as a caregiver of a special-needs child. This new lens has caused me to take notice of this incredible harshness within many of our personalities, right there under the surface. We may make comments about other people's misfortunes, without even thinking about who's listening, or how others could be devastated or depressed, as they try to make it through another day as a caregiver of a special-needs child. Here is what I mean.

I was beside-myself excited when, after being fairly persistent with the local soccer organization, I was able to get Connor signed up on a spring recreational soccer team. At 8 years old, this was his first experience in a team-oriented sport, though I knew and didn't care that he had not one ounce of competitive spirit in his body. To him, winning and losing didn't register. It was not important. Feelings were important. Is there a lesson here?

Connor was so proud to learn he was on a team with other boys who had the same color jersey. This was huge! The practices were trying. I attempted to keep him focused on what the coaches were trying to teach, since his typical attention span on any one thing can be in seconds, not minutes. It depends on what it is. But he was having so much fun being part of a team, a new experience for him.

At the first game, new orange jersey on and beaming from ear to ear, the coach called his name. *"Connor Boylan. You're a forward Connor. Get out there."*

Connor sprang to his feet as fast as I'd ever seen him, galloping onto the field, waving to everyone as if he was in the Rose Bowl Parade, yelping the whole way to the center of the field where the ref was standing. The ref blew the whistle and *Wham!* The ball was booted down the opposing team's field. All the boys took off running after it—all the boys except Connor. He stood there looking at the ref wondering if he was okay, since he had a frown on his face. Connor was concerned for him and immediately felt sad. In fact, he said, *"Are you okay?"* as parents and coaches were barking commands to their kids to go attack the ball.

Connor was oblivious to everything else going on. *"Get down there, Connor! Come on, Connor! Hustle, Connor! Go after the ball, Connor!"* the parents and coaches chanted. But Connor contently shadowed the ref as he moved around the field, focused on the ref's facial expression. Connor had no idea where the ball was, nor did he care. But it certainly seemed to irritate some of the parents. The coaches, who knew about his diagnosis of Williams, also seemed a bit irked, though they hid their frustration well. I mean, come on! It's about winning, right?

Some parents on the sidelines appeared confused. Others seemed visibly irritated that Connor hadn't blasted down the field with the other *normal* boys. I stood quietly behind them, some not knowing I was Connor's father. Then I heard one of the fathers say, "Look at that poor boy. He doesn't know *what's* going on. He doesn't get it. What's with that kid?"

At first blush, I wanted to go up to the guy, get in his face, and explain my son's situation so he felt like a raving idiot. But then I thought, surrender this one and let it go. So I did, at least I tried, though it made me angry and sad for the rest of the day. I couldn't get the tape to stop playing, "Look at that poor boy. He doesn't know *what's* going on."

Things like this happen frequently. I was going to have to learn how to let them slide off my shoulders as best I knew how, though it did make me angry when parents would say these things. Even when they learned Connor was my son, they *still* had a hard time keeping their comments to themselves. As I said, some folks are pretty harsh and very self-consumed. Winning is pretty important in our culture, just not to Connor. Feelings trump for him. These events are hard to shake off because they remind me of my son's challenges, though he's doing so well on many levels. Yet the fact remains, he is challenged, and always will be.

I am learning about when to speak up, and use it as a teaching point for those who aren't caregivers of special-needs children. I'm also learning when to keep my mouth shut, something much harder than you can imagine, at least, if you're a defender of your children, which most parents are.

This is an example of the harshness that routinely comes off many of our tongues. Maybe this is where the expression comes from, *"Bite your tongue."* It's a good expression, and one I'm trying to follow, since I've come to believe that unless people have had a life-altering situation hit them, many of us are clueless about being sensitive to the emotional and mental health needs of care-givers. Instead, we cast hurt without even thinking, which takes caregivers time and energy to work through. As if they don't have enough on their plates to deal with already!

As the title of this chapter asks, *What am I to learn from this?* I guess, to be more gentle and focused on the other person first. It's easy to say, but hard to do, unless there's a consequence. *"Poor boy?"* No. Lucky father? Yes! I didn't used to feel that way but I do now. Was I being taught something, and maybe, what to do with it?

What about you? What have you learned along your journey to this point? And have you figured out what to do with it, or where to apply it? It is worth pondering and discussing with other caregivers in your family, for certain. And with other friends who are caregivers.

Connor's first experience in a team sport. He was so proud. His first trophy!

Connor's first experience skiing. Resting at lunch–his favorite part!

CHAPTER SIXTEEN
ACCEPT THE SITUATION AND FIND PEACE WITH IT

Find peace with it? That's hard for anyone when things don't go their way. Us grownups are often the worst when things don't roll the way we think they should. And things hadn't rolled the right way for me for years. Did I feel excused from needing to find some peace with my new life? Absolutely! But acceptance of my new charter as the single father of a beautiful and challenging special-needs child was coming to a peaceful place of rest inside—a new grace that friends noticed. Actually, they thought I'd become *way too mellow*, suggesting I revert back to the old me. Not possible. This was the new person, necessary to cope with and manage the swings in Connor's day, activities and feelings. I had to stay loose, since I never knew when the next *thing* would hit. The *things* will change, of course, as he gets older, and I am already starting to experience that. Never a dull moment with The Boylan Boys.

Social graces are a concept that doesn't always register with Connor, though he is high functioning. He sometimes doesn't comprehend what's appropriate when, nor does he necessarily care. Remember, his brain is not *wired* like yours. He doesn't have the same number of genes. So trying to teach him various things—so he understands what is socially appropriate when and why—is often hard for him to grasp. To Connor, it's all about love, feelings, spontaneity and genuineness. Being honest and authentic registers. There is no other way to Connor. How wonderfully disarming actually. Still, it causes people pretty set in their ways to get uncomfortable. There's probably something to learn here as well.

Summer was here, which in Minnesota can mean it won't snow for at least another week. Weather people are a big hit in Minnesota since a normal conversation includes questions about what's in store weather-wise. This summery Saturday was gorgeous, and Connor and I were headed up to a friend's cabin for a day of relaxing, visiting, boating and eating with cousins and good friends, an annual event we looked forward to. Connor is a great traveler, listening to any piece of music I put on as he studies the patterns of each song. He has amazing rhythm.

The drive went by quickly and he blasted out of the Jeep yelling the names of his cousins, almost tackling them with his greeting. There were many fun people for Connor to chat and play with.

One particular man, I'll call him Bob, hadn't been there in years past so I don't think Connor had ever seen him before. A tremendous man, very accomplished, professional and formal, but that was his style. He was a kind and considerate man, always enjoyable to visit with. Remember, Connor doesn't understand personal or social boundaries very well at this stage in his life. After a fun day, Bob and his wife announced to everyone that they were going to head home. All of a sudden, Connor sprang to his feet, ran right at Bob, slamming into his legs, jolting him as he locked his arms around Bob's legs, saying at the top of his lungs, *"Bye, Bob. Love you, Bob."* Bob stood there surprised and stunned. Connor had invaded his personal space and touched him with his unfiltered love. You could see the surprise in Bob's eyes. It was a special moment—one I'm guessing Bob will never forget—how a challenged child broke through the formality and typical appropriate boundaries we all have to share some uncoached affection.

Would a *normal* child have done this? Maybe. Connor isn't affected by the rules of what's considered appropriate social behavior, and in this case, it seemed a welcomed and tender surprise that ended up touching someone. It is amazing how he has this impact on people though he's cognitively challenged. We can never have too much love, especially in this world.

"Bye, Bob. Love you, Bob." There will be many more situations like this one in the years ahead, some pleasant and special like this one, others that will be tough to handle, based on whatever he does. And I will be there to witness the good intentions and how they will be received. And since I don't have much of a choice in the matter anyway, accepting these situations as they happen,

then finding peace with them, regardless of what happens, is about the only way I know of to attempt to remain calm and balanced—maybe even learn a thing or two from my special-needs Angel Child.

The Cowboy Hoedown at the T-Lazy-7 Ranch

CHAPTER SEVENTEEN
WHERE'S THE HUMOR?

We all need humor. Sometimes, it's the only thing that can help us make it through. Yet for years, humor had hidden its face from me. I couldn't find any, in anything—a good comedy, a funny movie or a clown at the circus. **Nothing** was funny anymore. Life was a series of serious events, usually draining and tough. Yet as I came to accept and find peace with my new life, the humor came from Connor. Sometimes not appropriate, but always genuine and harmless.

For example, one of my close friends and his wife referred their European cleaning lady and her company to me. They said she was a trustworthy person who had done a great job, so I thought I'd give her and her two helpers a try.

Never having met them, Connor ran to the front door of the house as a blond woman and two darker-haired ladies meekly approached carry vacuum cleaners, mops and cleaning supplies. Once on the stoop, they looked through the glass front doors, waiting patiently for him to let them in. Jumping up and down as if he'd never seen people before, Connor ripped open the front door, smiled and said, "Hello girls. Want to sleep over in my bed today?"

Not knowing about Connor, the blond glared at me, like I was some weirdo who couldn't be trusted. As if I'd put Connor up to saying such a thing!

I gently apologized, explaining that my son had special needs. They shrugged it off after they began to engage with him and realized that something about him was different, and oh so genuine.

Humor had to come back now for the sake of my own mental health, because life was even harder and more intense. Humor would have to be my new leveler, my chill-out gauge and my barometer for finding a new pace with Connor. Humor was also something I used all the time to help him when he'd get stuck, a common occurrence.

Similar to someone with Alzheimer's, which I'm familiar with since I helped take care of my father's parents in their later years, Connor can be functioning at a high level and all of a sudden, he'll freeze. It's as if his brain goes dark, locks up or goes on strike for a moment. I'll get the deer-in-the-headlights look, and know immediately what's going on. It's like he goes away momentarily, and sometimes, it's as if he doesn't know it's happening. Everything just stops—and then he'll come back. In these times, I remain calm with humor at the ready, which sometimes helps pull him back from wherever he went for a while.

Where's the humor in my own story? There isn't any really, but it's being offered up to you and others who may or may not be a caregiver, with the hope that by sharing it, others will find solace and hope as they manage through the sometimes intensely difficult times caregivers can face throughout their lifetime. And to acknowledge that without humor or being able to *find* humor in our darkest hours, then we *are* in trouble. It's that important to our mental health and overall desire to move forward. This is very important to heed as a caregiver of a special-needs child. Humor is often the only thing that provides temporary relief—maybe even makes us laugh, at the situation, at our special-needs child, or at ourselves. And since plain-old laughter evidently helps us mentally, why not find as much humor as you can? That's my gig!

Connor often does very funny things as he goes about his day, and what makes them so special is that **he's not trying to be funny**, but real. And *that* is the coolest part for me. The unbridled rawness of real!

Gretchen, one of Connor's ski instructors at Challenge Aspen

Beverly, one of Connor's ski instructors at Challenge Aspen

Christmas morning—Santa ate the cookie we left out for him!

LAYING NEW CEMENT—MANAGING THE SETBACKS WITH GRACE

At 54 years old, I'm starting over in one sense. But in another, I have a story meant to uplift others experiencing similar struggles over mind, heart and their **desire** to move forward as they care for their special-needs children, or deal with another intense time calling for massive strength.

Whereas I thought I had a solid foundation under me, it seems that for some reason (which I believe will be revealed in the years ahead), it's been busted up with a jackhammer, as I lay down fresh cement underneath my new life to create a foundation that will be more secure and enduring as it hardens up underneath a more empathetic heart. And the setbacks? There have been many; so many and so frequent that it felt as though I was being used for target practice on a never-ending manhunt, until I turned myself over to someone who I believe has been hunting me for a long time. Perhaps to do more important work for the benefit of many in need.

I'll manage the setbacks ahead—and there will be plenty—as Connor grows and experiences life. And I am now focused on assisting caregivers (who may be wondering if they'll *ever* get any relief) of special-needs children in the trenches day in and day out. I've been there—am there—and know what it feels like. Helping them make it through seems a worthwhile endeavor. And at the end of the day, isn't *this* what it's all about—helping others get over the humps in life to a better place?

If you're not a caregiver, **how will you help** those who are? Surely you can do something, especially for those caregivers that live in your neighborhood, or that you know through your church, your work or some other association. So **what will you do** for them? And if you **are** a caregiver, join **The Reach For Me Network** so you begin getting the support, encouragement and inspiration you need, from other like-minded caregivers of special-needs children, regardless of the diagnosis of the child or children—cognitive or physical, since we share so much in common. We can all help one another, which *is* the grand design.

CHAPTER NINETEEN
MOVING FORWARD—THE PICTURES AHEAD

When everything hit for me, I couldn't see anything forward. Perhaps it is or was that way for you. There were no pictures ahead, as I mentioned. Just fog so thick you could have cut it with a knife. There was no clear direction for which way my boat should sail, as there was no wind. But with grace and guidance, I was brought through the fire. The refiner's fire, as this one particular book talks about. I've got some nice burns, but nothing I haven't learned to handle if I'm centered and calm.

Can I tell you that all the flames have been put out? No, they haven't. There are still some that are smoldering as I look for new pictures and new experiences with Connor that I believe will create the path ahead. Is this approach too fuzzy? Not at all, as I am done attempting to forge ahead solely with my own plan, without the guidance and grace from above, helping show me and reinforce the right way to go.

I've hit *way* too many cement walls over the past several years to forge ahead without asking for guidance. If that's too mushy for you, I understand. But for me, it's how I've come to learn that someone else is ultimately in charge, and that I need to do a better job of listening to that voice and following through with what I hear. Again, not exactly the Type A, kick-butt and take-some-names personality that I learned was critically important in the business world, but rather, perhaps a wiser approach. Involving Him in my planning by asking for guidance and then actually trying to listen for the answers. Something I can honestly say I wasn't doing a whole bunch of for the first 25 years.

Again, if that is too mushy for you, that's okay. I'm just sharing what I've learned. However, what I believe at this point, after all the hardship and knowing there are more tough times ahead, is that if we just have the faith to ask—and then listen—we will be shown how to make it through. It's like a steady light guiding you along day by day, as you're ready to walk just a little bit farther, to a place where you *know* you'll be all right—that you *can* do it! And that you *will* do it! You will move forward creating new and better pictures ahead for you, your special-needs child or children, and your family. Not because you have no choice in the matter, because you do! But perhaps you've never considered this perspective, as I never did when I was thrashing around for answers for years.

Perhaps YOU have been called! Called for an *extra* level of service to and for your special-needs children, or someone dear to you. And through your service and care and all that you put forth, you'll be given an understanding of life and love that is so deep and so real, that you will feel the hand of the Almighty on your shoulder as he looks you in the face and says, *"You can do this. You will do this. I will give you the strength you need and it will come from the love and care you give to your Angel Child."*

There are new pictures ahead for you! You will create them as your new life unfolds. Believe that. I have, and continue to feel the warmth of that belief, because it does help you move forward. So trust that perhaps **you** have been given a **special dispensation**—an Angel Child—and that you are already closer than most to seeing what the face and hands of the Creator feel like, as you open up to and embrace the new pictures that are in store for you. Be blessed—and hold your Angel Child.

Connor played the banker
in Mary Poppins at Camp

Signing in for
music and dance camp

CHAPTER TWENTY

THE CONNOR PRINCIPLES™—GUIDEPOSTS FOR EVERYDAY LIFE

In any tragedy, hardship or traumatic event, there are lessons that can be taken away from the situation and hopefully applied in the times ahead. Sometimes these lessons don't come all at once, but rather, are revealed over time; maybe as we're ready to receive, understand and do something with them, so we don't make the same mistakes again. Or perhaps it's so that we adjust ourselves for the times ahead, becoming stronger, wiser and deeper, with a more complete perspective from the experience. Maybe to help someone else headed into a similar situation we are in, or have already been through.

That said, I was sitting in a lawn chair reflecting on all that had happened— yellow notepad in my lap, pencil in hand, just as my aunt, the Carmelite Nun, had encouraged me to do. I was staring out over the ocean during a gorgeous sunset, asking for guidance and relief, when these principles, the ones I am about to share with you, came gushing into my head. I didn't have to figure them out, organize them into a manner that made sense, or even name them. They came that way—in a specific order, each with their own key point and three-word slogan, making them easy to remember. The 10 came in one conscious stream—that fast! I needed to get myself out of the way and not micromanage the information, since it was coming from the best communicator of information the world has ever known. Better not mess with that.

I let the information flow onto the paper in the manner it seemed designed, to teach, comfort and bring hope, so that when applied, they could actually manifest these things for others. And I believe they will, with trust and belief in the person who brought them to and through me—to you! Intense? Not really. Powerful? Yes. Simple? That's their beauty.

As you read *The Connor Principles™*, remember who they're ultimately coming from, and let them be of comfort to you in your current situation and the future. Remember the passages from Rick Warren's book *The Purpose Driven Life*:

*"God uses problems to draw you closer to himself. The Bible says, The Lord is close to the brokenhearted; he rescues those who are crushed in spirit. Your most profound and intimate experiences of worship will likely be in your darkest days—when your heart is broken, when you feel abandoned, when you're out of options, when the pain is great—and you turn to God alone. It is during suffering that we learn to pray our most authentic, heartfelt, honest-to-God prayers. Problems force us to look to God and depend on him instead of ourselves. **You'll never know that God is all you need until God is all you've got!***

*There's a Grand Designer behind everything. Your life is not a result of random chance, fate, or luck. There is a master plan. God is pulling the strings. God's plan for your life involves all that happens to you—including your mistakes, your sins, and your hurts. Under **pressure**, your faith-life is forced into the open and shows its true colors."*

Another Easter Bunny

Enjoying Cowboy Hoedown
at T-Lazy-7 Ranch

CONNOR PRINCIPLE ONE
RELEASE THE ANGER

Bullying! Now there is a word that causes most of us to get pretty riled up, since the mere sound of the word can get anyone's blood pressure elevated. The visions most of us have of total unfairness are strong and come to the surface quickly when we experience or even hear about such behavior. Just the thought of teasing or tormenting children considered "normal" who might be defenseless gets most people ready to come out swinging at those who would do such a thing. And for those that use this type of behavior on children who they *know* are indeed special needs, well, perhaps they need some harsh punishment so they never behave this way again, period. Parents and school administrators top to bottom need to be informed as well, so this type of behavior is halted, and fast. At least that is my "old-fashioned" set of beliefs. It needs to be dealt with firmly, quickly, decisively, and with genuinely harsh consequences for those who bully, so they clearly get the message the first time that it is unacceptable! Unfortunately, those of us who are parents of special-needs children deal with this from time to time, perhaps more than we care to admit. It is actually quite sickening. And people wonder why parents of special-needs children are sometimes on edge. We've got lots to watch out for in advocating for our children. Lots.

Therefore, you can understand how I felt—maybe just a *bit* angry—or maybe more, when, for several days, Connor came home from summer school and was unusually quiet. He wasn't himself. He was going directly to his room, closing the door, sitting with Snuffy, holding her, rocking back and forth more than normal, tears coming down his cheeks, not willing to tell me what was wrong as he feared the boys who were teasing him would get in trouble. Let's just say that I had heard enough. I called the supervisor, staff members and anyone else who would listen, inquiring as to if they were aware, and if so, what did they know, not know, etc. I was on an urgent fact-finding mission of the highest importance, ready to kick someone's ass, to be frank. What was the first Connor Principle again? Release The Anger? And once I learned who the boys were, maintaining my cool was hard to do. I wanted access to their parents as well, to share my thoughts of disgust, as I felt, right or wrong, that they were "bad" parents, not doing their job properly. I mean, what child would bully another? I *know* you can relate.

We got the whole situation under control quickly, the boys involved were reprimanded, and the matter subsided quickly, though naturally, it took Connor a while before he would go around those boys again. And he felt very sad since he feels things on such a deep level. This little incident is one of many types of situations that we, as parents of special-needs children, may encounter frequently throughout our lifetime. It's natural to get angry, because something is happening to your own "flesh and blood." Not only do you feel justified in your anger, but that anger can almost manifest in you wanting to take actions that might not be healthy for you, your special-needs child, or your family.

I don't care who you are, how accomplished you might be, your place in society, or how strong you might be as a person. When the news hits that you have a child or children with special needs—perhaps *profound* special needs, and that it may **forever** alter your life moving forward in various ways, you *are* going to get frustrated and mad! Downright angry, in fact! This story is one example of what I mean. No matter how reserved or introverted your personality and temperament, you *will* get angry. If you disagree or feel I'm overblowing the situation, it's perhaps because you're not being that honest with yourself yet. *Every* parent that gets ***the news*** that his or her child or children has a diagnosed special-need, goes through a process of digesting the news. Some do a better job of digesting it than others, but no one is practiced at it. How could you be? And at some point in that process, trust me—**anger will show up on multiple fronts!**

It's okay to get angry and frustrated. For crying out loud, what's wrong with that, when you receive news that your child might or does have a special-needs diagnosis? It's news that will beyond a shadow of a doubt, alter, change or prevent some or many of the dreams, expectations and goals you've had for your life from perhaps **ever** being realized. That's a pretty good reason to get angry. It's more than a slight curve ball you've been thrown. It's a curve ball that never stops curving! More like a knuckle ball since, with a special-needs child, you often don't know what's coming next.

Now that we've established that you're going to get angry, incredibly anxious and frustrated numerous times over the years to come, and that it's okay to feel that way about the situations life has handed you, learning how to **deal with** and **release** these thoughts and emotions is not only important, but essential to your own mental health going forward—and that of your family's.

That said—do I have some special formula or time-tested *process* that will help release the anger? Absolutely not. It is something I struggle with as well. Everyone has to find their own way in which they can essentially release the anger and frustrations that come with life-altering news about a special-needs child; the shock and numbness you feel, the sense of hopelessness, despair and sadness. Then there are also all of the new realities that have to be faced over time, that you may never again have the life you've had up until the time of the diagnosis. It's a whole new ball game now, with new players, new situations to deal with, and lots to learn and figure out. (On the flipside, there are the new-found joys that also come over time.)

Is it selfish to be angry when you get the news? Who cares? You may have received incredibly difficult news that may take *years* to digest. Yes, years. I am still digesting the news about Connor's diagnosis, and it's been years. I still find myself in scenarios where I'm bothered about something I can't do because of my life as a caregiver of a special-needs child. Is that selfish? Sure, but I don't beat myself up about it; nor should you! Cut yourself some slack once in a while. It is hard! And it might be hard for a while, or for the rest of your life! No one really knows, which is frustrating, because most of us like to know **exactly** what we're looking at in terms of what the future holds. With a special-needs child, those answers are sometimes hard to come by. Therefore, finding yourself frustrated, in an anxious state, angry or downright beside yourself is not at all difficult to understand. Here's another reason caregivers need to stick together, to help one another through these legitimate feelings. "Stuffing" the anger, something I believe men are pretty accomplished at, is a dumb move, as it helps no one and can actually do damage.

What I'm learning is that I'll probably have these feelings from time to time for the rest of my life, that it's okay, and that I need to learn how to cope with and manage them in order to stay focused on my son. I need to remain **optimistic** to the future as he grows and changes, and remember that I've been *called* (maybe you've been called too) for an extra level of service, which you can't deliver if you're angry all the time. This deep-seated belief has helped me cope and manage. Maybe it will help you too.

Anger can be dangerous to you, your friends, family, coworkers and your special-needs children. So, for their sake and yours, find some help if you or others close to you feel you need it, so you can release it. Sometimes, the only people able to comprehend how hard and lonely it is being a caregiver are other caregivers. They get it—the pain, frustration, anxiety, loneliness and sense of loss. They also struggle, as I do, with not wanting to come across as a **complainer**. This is precisely why so many of us keep to ourselves; we don't want to come across as a complainer. Instead, we figure it's best not to share what our lives are *really* like, as some of us think, "Who would believe me if I told them what my life was *really* like?" Yet we'd also like to have a *life* once in a while, since it's normal to feel as though ours was radically altered, driving feelings of anxiety, stress and yes, ANGER! Fellow caregivers *get* the anger and anxiety thing and the importance of needing to release it.

Releasing the anger can bring a new level of peace and acceptance about all the unknowns that lie ahead, so you can handle them in stride, growing deeper, more resilient and stronger. You'll be more helpful to other caregivers as well. Therefore, find a way to release it, over, and over, and over again. Make it part of your daily regime so that you *can* move forward.

PERSONAL REFLECTIONS SECTION AFTER EACH CONNOR PRINCIPLE

The books I have read over the years, be they Christian or faith-based, self-help or business, that have helped me think through and summarize key points and how they may apply to my life, are the ones that have helped me the most, by far. This is especially true if I am trying to change some aspect of my life for myself, or for others. That is why I have added the **Personal Reflections Summary** to the end of each of The Connor Principles. Why? To help! That's why.

As a caregiver of a special-needs child (or adult), many of us already know that based on the diagnosis of our child and where they are in their overall progress and life skills, we will be dealing with significant issues until either we pass on—or they do. There's no other way to say it. It is what it is, as many people like to say. Because of this rather significant and ever-present "situation" in our lives, the emotional, psychological, spiritual and financial hills and valleys we must go through can sometimes be intense. And this is precisely what The Connor Principles are for: to help take the edge off, **reduce** our levels of **anxiety, doubt, stress, fear** and **worry**, find a deeper meaning or **perspective** to it all, chill out a bit, or develop a deeper level of **faith** when there doesn't appear to be many good options. Funny how our faith-life is **forced** out into the open when we are in troubled waters. It is often the raw truth, for men and women alike—that until we are in dire need of an answered prayer (or two or three!), we rarely, if ever, spend the time that perhaps we ought to, focused on being grateful and saying thank you. You might be thinking, *"Be grateful for what? My life is just plain hard! It would be a tall order if you think I'm going to get on my knees and give thanks for what's going on in my life right now."* Most of our energies seem to go toward making a living and providing for our families. Right or wrong, it's just the way life works out for most of us.

This Personal Reflections Summary is your opportunity to spend some time reflecting on and discussing whatever is on your **mind** and **heart** regarding each one of The Connor Principles and how they appear or are realized in your own life, at home and at work, on your journey as a caregiver of a special-needs child. This is helpful for **all** caregivers—women and **men**, who are typically not considered the caregiver type, let alone capable. So if you're a man, I suggest you **not attempt** to **escape**, kick down the road, or put off what could be a beneficial exercise for you as well, serving you, your spouse and your family in constructive ways going forward. Why would anyone want to escape, or not take seriously, real-life *stuff* that might be going on in your own life right now—with yourself, your spouse or significant other, your immediate and/or extended family, and/or with things at work? Why?

At the end of each chapter going forward there are questions designed for your own **reflection** and maybe for **discussion**—with your spouse, significant other, or another caregiver, so you have some level of shared experience and mutual empathy. You might choose someone from your book club, movie group, exercise group, running club, cooking club, church group, Bible study or your work. It's your call. The important thing is that you "Just Do It," as the Nike commercials so plainly state. Connect with another caregiver or two, if not your spouse or significant other, to talk these things through—these emotions, feelings and issues, whatever they might be. **Each principle** is designed to be a platform for your own internal reflections around each one; how you could reduce your own stress, anxiety, doubt and worry, and find a deeper, more helpful perspective that will assist you in finding a new level of faith, courage, strength or self-empowerment. These principles can truly improve your quality of life if you are willing to use and apply them as part of your daily routine! That's what this is about! This is where the **sharing** of **your caregiver journey** will perhaps—surprisingly to you—help someone else on theirs.

Caring for the caregiver—the simple mantra of The Reach For Me Network. It's about reaching out to fellow caregivers and helping one another, since we've got much in common to deal with and manage, and to be grateful for, though it is hard to be grateful for what is on our plates from time-to-time. I understand that. But it doesn't mean we ought to stop trying to be grateful, or helping each other.

One last thought. Remember that the questions in each Personal Reflections Section are not designed to upset, irritate or annoy you. Rather, they are there to help you reflect on how your situation affects you, your family and perhaps, your life at work. They are designed to help you look deeper and **honestly** at whatever you feel needs to be looked at, discussed or dealt with, in relation to each one of the principles and how they could, through their daily use and embrace, help enrich the quality of your life, and that of your family. This is my humble hope and desire. So, are you ready? I hope so. Here we go on the questions around Personal Reflections for Connor Principle One—Release The Anger. Grab a **notepad** or **journal** and **write down** your thoughts and answers—a good way to go through each principle. Or, write them down right here if you prefer. Whatever works.

Personal Reflections Around Connor Principle One– Release The Anger

As a caregiver of a special-needs child, there's plenty we can get wound up about from time to time, if we're being honest. For example, the status of our marital relationship or relationship with a significant other, if we're in one, or the lack thereof, because whomever we might be interested in might not want to engage in the added level of stress or "complications" around a life with a special-needs child.

Consider your family life, your work life, and the dreams or goals that might be delayed—or might not happen at all now. Think about interactions with extended family members and how they do or don't wish to *get involved* or help out once in a while, because they don't really view it as their *job* since they're just "extended family." Think about your health insurance provider or providers, doctors, specialists, therapists, nutritionists, school administrators, lawyers, special education teachers, your child's paraprofessional, and a hundred other things; just pick a few and begin. **Answer these Personal Reflection Questions** as best you can, then **discuss them** with those you feel they should be discussed with. It will help!

1) What would others, such as your spouse, a close friend or a co-worker, say you are stressed, anxious or angry about in relation to your special-needs child and your life as a caregiver?

2) What is on your mind or heart in regard to this Connor Principle— Release The Anger?

3) What is bothering, frustrating or challenging you in regard to this principle that you feel needs to be dealt with, discussed, improved and/or resolved? With whom?

4) Why are these things or issues bothering, frustrating or challenging you? What are **you** not getting?

5) What are your suggestions for coping, dealing with, improving or resolving these issues or challenges?

6) Which solutions to these issues or challenges will work out best in your opinion, and why?

7) How will you commit to do the work, either yourself or with your significant other, family or another caregiver, to Release The Anger—however that shows up in you as a caregiver?

Once you write down your thoughts and reflections; talk them through with those involved in your caregiving journey, be it another caregiver, your spouse/significant other, an immediate or extended family member, a close friend, etc. Then commit to **come back** to these things **every week** for three to four months or more, to revisit your progress on each topic you wish to work on, improve or resolve. Your goal is to reduce stress, worry, fear and anxiety, and improve the peace and contentment within yourself and your family regarding this principle—Release The Anger.

Anger can be toxic to you and **everyone** else around you, so **get rid of it** as best you can, and move forward with a newfound sense of purpose, spirit and empowerment.

Enjoying a jazz concert
on Snowmass Mountain

Walking home after
skating together

BLOCK THE DOUBTING

As I mentioned, doubt, or worse yet, self-doubt, which can come upon you out of nowhere when you receive life-altering news, is not only a paralyzing drug, but one that can stop your life in its tracks on all levels. And *that* hurts your special-needs children and your family.

NOBODY—no self-help guru, television talk-show personality, motivational speaker, prince, princess, president, queen, king, ambassador, professional actor, athlete or the like, has any better *fix* or approach on handling doubt or self-doubt than you or me. In fact, here's a unique way to consider things: perhaps as caregivers of special-needs children, we have had more than our fair share of surprises and life interruptions. And because of this, we've been *forced* to deal with more intense levels of self-doubt than others. So maybe *we* are better prepared than most to cope with it when it arises. It's something worth considering, since many of us have had to wrestle with so much of it on an ongoing basis, throughout the course of our lives as caregivers.

Doubt, like anger, can essentially ruin your life because it can strip away the joy sitting right in front of you for you to experience through your special-needs child. But if you're all hosed up inside, you're locked out from experiencing anything. You **must** find a way to release the doubts that may have filled your head and heart, to someone who has more power than us all.

Do I have doubts? Absolutely. And so do you! No need to play big man on campus as if you're unaffected. They are part of our everyday existence. So learning to somehow block them as best we can from overtaking your person is critically important in helping you accept and embrace the new life that lies ahead, with all its twists and turns.

As I write this particular story, Connor is in the eight grade, academically functioning at a third–grade level based on the particular test scores you look at. I am so proud of the progress he is making, as he works very hard. He still has a full-time paraprofessional with him during the school day to help him focus and transition from one thing to the next, as he is a delightful social creature who would prefer to chat the day away on topics of **ultra** high importance to him: the leaf blower, the weed-whacker, mowers, the mail, candy, Halloween costumes, his drums, music, etc.

Connor has several fixations, some of which I've mentioned, which can be intense if you're not in the right mind-set. They are based on his maniacal focus on certain things and the challenge is to move him **off** of these things gracefully once he has *locked on*. As a parent of a special-needs child, I *know* you can relate. It seems that many—or maybe *most*—special-needs children have certain things they obsess over, fixate on, or get stuck on, depending on the diagnosis of the child. As if you or I don't have any quirks or issues? Anyway, whatever your special-needs child's particular fixations are—or the things that *must* be part of their routine, it is understandable why we, as parents, sometimes have to stand back and somehow find some **humor** in it all. Otherwise, it is quite easy to go nuts! This is one area where the doubting can take you over. Doubting because—based on the fixation and the constant, almost obsessive need they can have to do certain things over, and over, and over, and over, it is easy to kind of stand outside of yourself and think, *"Look at me, doing this or that. I can't believe **my life**! This is nuts. Am I going to be doing this with my child for the next five or 10 years?"*

Here is an example of what I mean, and why frequent bouts of intense doubting are common among us, encouraging us to find some way of keeping our **humor** at the **ready**, or remain light-hearted in times when you are being tested via various routines or fixations your special-needs child may have as part of what makes them happy and fulfilled.

It was the summer of 2012 and Connor was almost 14 years old. I'd just picked him up from his Club Care summer school session, which he really liked. We were heading home in the Jeep as I began laying out our schedule for the evening, as he still needs to understand what activities come next and in what order. Heaven forbid I need to change up the order for whatever reason! When that happens, it adds to the evening's (or morning's or afternoon's) hills and valleys. Anyway, when we got home, he **methodically** went about his routine of heading to the mailbox to check the mail, which I am **not** to touch. (I can't even go near the mailbox—only him.) So once that dance was completed to his satisfaction, he headed straight for the BLOWER! His gas-powered leaf blower gives him over-the-moon satisfaction from (as he calls it) pumping the starter (translation, pulling the cord to start the blower), then turning it off, then pulling the cord again, then turning if off, then pulling it again, then turning if off. He usually repeats this pattern until I am convinced the damn thing is going to blow up or fall apart. The manufacturer should consider hiring Connor as a product destruction specialist or tester of some sort, as his fixations around blowers and weed-whackers, the sounds they make, along with the wonderful vibrations he feels from holding them are something he lives for. Like daily— or at the very least, every other day! Lucky me! **You try it** sometime, and try and keep your humor face on **and** stay calm. I'll buy you a hamburger if you can do it!

Anyway, once he went through his start, stop, start, stop, start, and stop routine for a period of time, he finally let the blower run for a while. So there he goes in all his glory: shorts hanging down, mirror sunglasses on, his red sound-deadening headphones on to minimize the noise, which I don't get since he loves the sound of the blower but still wants them on, his 3M mask to minimize the dirt and dust in his lungs, face and eyes, and his rubber-reinforced work gloves. Got the picture? He's a man on a mission to blow whatever is in his path; rocks, the mailbox, shrubs, trees, the grass, a pile of dirt in the backyard, the garage door, the side of the house, or the hood of the Jeep! In Connor's world, **nothing is off limits** from the blower. It is the one lawn maintenance tool he **cannot** do without.

Happy to use the blower until the gas runs out, he took off for the backyard to blow some dirt by the retaining wall as I went inside to check my emails, and maybe, get a phone call or two in before making dinner. I always have to have my eye on him when he's in "blower heaven" as he **loses himself** in what he is doing. He will roam all over the place once he's got the blower in his hands. It's not uncommon for him to blow the neighbor's rocks, bushes, grass, the siding on their house, their garage door, or even their car, if it's in the driveway. The neighbors don't much appreciate this, of course, which is why there's **no downtime** for me when he's in blower mode. Instead, I'm on high alert. This particular day, I had him in sight from the living room, as he was blowing this pile of dirt: there was dirt flying up in his face and all around. Quite a sight, but he was happy as a clam. I usually give him 20 to 30 minutes of blower time. hoping he'll get his "fix" in that amount of time, because that's about **all** I can handle, if you want the truth.

All of a sudden, I couldn't see him in the backyard. I went through the kitchen door to the garage, and there he was, standing in front of the Jeep in the driveway. Blower running, he had turned the blower hose on his own face, trying to cool himself down, gasoline leaking out and running down his leg, though he had no clue, since he was sweating like a pig, dirt all over his face, arms and legs. I ran toward him, grabbed the blower, shut it off, and *tried* to show him the gas running down his leg. Let's just say that *wasn't* the right way to handle the situation, at least in Connor's mind. He was furious I had taken the blower from him without asking. He threw his sound-deadening headphones onto the driveway, cracking them, tore off his 3M mask, ripped off his work gloves, yelled at me, stormed in the house, into his room, and slammed the door so hard the pictures on the other side of the wall came off their hooks, falling to the floor. I had *never* seen Connor this worked up before, ever! And I was nervous because he could not calm himself down—another first. I bear-hugged him from the front, trying to help him take deep some breaths, but to no avail. He was *so mad* he couldn't calm himself down. It was a bit scary. It was as if he was obsessed with the thing! I felt like leaving it out in the street so someone would run over it, steal it, or the garbage man would take it. But then I'd just have to buy another one.

I left him in his room, door closed, me sitting right outside his door listening. After about 20 minutes of crying, fussing and hitting the pillows on his bed, I heard him start talking to Snuffy, his blankly. Remember—Snuffy is a real person to Connor—still. She's from Mexico, he says. She's a bird, she has wings, and she has children, though I've not yet met any of them. He started telling Snuffy that I was in trouble for taking the blower, and that I was a bad Daddy. He talked to her for about 20 minutes, which was fine, because it was calming him down. Then he came out of his room, sat down next to me and said, *"I think you're having a hard day. I think you're confused, Daddy. That's not right you took my blower. It's just not right."* I was clearly in the wrong, and if I *ever* did that again, I would be in serious trouble. All of my explaining as to why I did it fell on deaf and confused ears, since this was his BLOWER.

I was exhausted. I made dinner, cleaned him up, and put him to bed early, as I was spent. I lay in bed almost numb, wondering if I was going to have lots more of these episodes in the near future because of his compulsive need for the blower to be in his hands as much as possible. I'd never seen Connor like this before—the opposite of the sweet, easy-going, mild-mannered, kind, happy and polite boy I was raising him to be.

The day ended with me being stressed out, on edge, and **filled with doubt** about how many more of these experiences were ahead, and whether I could control him when they happened. And if not, what were my options?

Block The Doubting—Connor Principle Two. Easy to talk about and quite another to do. But very important to do, in whatever manner works best. It's as relevant as releasing the anger, so you don't burn yourself out. If that happens, you're no good to yourself, your special-needs child, spouse or your family. So coming up with some sort of "process" to minimize or avoid all the areas where doubt could show up is something worth proactively doing. It will help protect your own mental health, which affects your **life span**. And since we're all interested in hanging around for as long as possible, it's smart to come up with your own plan around this principle, so you can Block The Doubting as you feel it coming upon you on your caregiver journey.

The lyrics to the caregiver anthem song *Angel Child* came into my head from the visual of Connor pawing my forehead as we sat on the floor in our living room and him kind of saying, "Reach For Me, it's going to be okay. The peace is in me. Just reach for me." Consider sitting with your special-needs child by yourself sometime and getting some of the peace that it seems many of them have inside. This has helped me in my times of intense doubt, to gain perspective and patience.

Another proud class graduation moment

Personal Reflections Around Connor Principle Two
Block The Doubting

It's important to reflect upon the following questions regarding how this principle shows up in your life as a caregiver. Write down your thoughts, and ask others involved in the caregiving to do the same. Then discuss them together, or with another caregiver who might be dealing with similar challenges. You never know how sharing your own challenges and journey will help another caregiver. Helping others helps us feel better about things and puts us in a better place. Here are the questions to reflect upon and discuss:

1) Write a paragraph or two about what your life was like before you had a special-needs child.

2) Write a paragraph or two about what your life is like now with a special-needs child, and three ways in which it has changed for you, good, bad or indifferent.

3) What dreams or goals are you unable to achieve now, or perhaps ever?

4) What is the best way to deal/cope with these things?

5) What does your special-needs child do or not do that makes you stressed out, anxious or annoyed that brings on the doubt? What can you do when these things happen to help minimize the doubt? This is important, as it's connected to maintaining good mental health so we can function at our best, for ourselves and our special-needs children.

6) What are the biggest doubts you have about the future with your special-needs child?

Celebrating his 8th year
at music & dance camp

Having a chat during lunch
and working me for candy

ACCEPT THE LOVE

How nice would it be if we could learn to accept another person's love when it doesn't come in the form or fashion we think it should—a gesture of appreciation or affection toward us without trying to control, filter or micromanage how it is shown? That would be a huge lesson, though merely just a fantasy, being how concerned most of us are about how things *look* and the *appearance* of this or that needing to be just so—at least in our opinion. And you thought most of us weren't interested in control. Think that one through again!

This is another big lesson from Connor's world. He is cognitively challenged with his diagnosis of Williams, though high functioning in many areas at the present time. And as he continues to grow, he may continue to make great strides in certain areas, or he may not. I don't really know, and nor do any medical doctors. It will be what it will be. But Connor understands one thing very well—giving love unconditionally. He doesn't understand nor comprehend the concept of a stranger, or why anyone would be mean or disrespectful to him. There is no such thing in his world. Everyone is a friend who should be loved. Another reason it is easy for me to worry, as he has no comprehension around why anyone would want to do him harm. It simply doesn't register.

I have watched him approach people he's never seen before with the warmest of greetings, only to watch many of these people (mostly adults) not accept his warmth, but rather, angle in on what's wrong with him. Accept his love? No. They're trying to figure out what's the matter with him. And the love? It goes right by them. It was intended for them, no question there. But they couldn't accept it. Why? I wish I knew. Are *you* like that? Can you accept the love from your own special-needs child? And if you aren't a parent of a special-needs child, are you able to accept the love they show you when you encounter them? If not, go hang out with some special-needs children in your area tomorrow, and they'll quickly teach you what it's all about, though they're just being themselves. Interesting what we can all learn from children born with *less* than what we have, in one sense.

Connor's biggest, most important, all-encompassing holiday (to date) is Halloween! Christmas just doesn't compare. Why do you suppose this is? Because it involves one of his key fixations at the present time—candy! Yes, it is big! A good couple of months **prior** to Halloween, he begins his ritual of donning his full-blown costume—which he calls his "scary ghost mask"—in front of the bathroom mirror. The ensemble includes a floor-length black flowing, silky cape, black gloves and a white scary ghost mask. He puts on his costume, mounts his bike and rides around the neighborhood, waving to everyone as if his costume just won "Best in Class" at the International Costume Show. This ritual usually begins around July, before anyone expects to encounter a child in Halloween garb. He is **so happy** as he rides around in his costume, waving, as people are thinking, *"What in the H... is that?"* Can they accept the love? Hardly. More likely they are wondering why he's doing such a crazy thing **three months early**! Too bad we often can't experience the simple joy that our special-needs children feel about simple things, no matter how crazy they might seem to us. There's definitely a lesson here.

Good or bad, many special-needs children don't know how to worry. It doesn't register with them. They know love. It's what they understand and give. And maybe, just maybe, we could all be happier and more comforted if we learned, as these children already know, how to accept the love. **It is there for you** to experience, from your **own** special-needs child, even in the times you might be going through right now. Accept it, and find a new level of peace more powerful than *any* drug.

PERSONAL REFLECTIONS AROUND CONNOR PRINCIPLE THREE
ACCEPT THE LOVE

Reflect upon the following questions regarding how this principle shows up in your life as a caregiver. Write down your thoughts, and ask others involved in the caregiving to do the same. Then discuss them together, or with another caregiver who might be dealing with similar challenges. Here are the questions to consider and discuss:

1) Are you able to accept the love from your special-needs child? Consider asking your spouse/significant other, another family member, friend or co-worker to answer before you to see how their answers compare with yours.

2) If you are not a caregiver of a special-needs child, are you able to accept their love when you encounter them?

3) What's blocking you from being able to accept their love?

4) If you are struggling in this area, do you want to change so you are able to accept their love? How?

christmas morning, 2012

Christmas break, 2012 skiing
together--he's growing up

GIVE TO GIVE

As I've mentioned, Connor has approached people he's never seen before with open arms and a total trust in them, wanting to greet them, hug them, give them something—only to be rejected in more than a few cases. Rebuffed and shunned. It is hard to watch. He'll look at me with total confusion. But he doesn't really comprehend (at his current stage of development) the notion of being rejected, so he'll often come right back at the person who has rejected his gestures with the same heartfelt intent of wanting to give them his greeting and whatever else he was intending to give.

Giving to give for the simple genuine tenderness of giving. It has taken people aback, and melted away their defensiveness. What power. Giving to give.

Connor doesn't understand lashing back at people if they don't receive him kindly, something I dare say many of us are pretty good at, if we're being honest. Maybe this is because when he's giving, he isn't looking to **get something** in return. There's no expectation there. By watching him give to give, I have seen him melt away the snarls, hurt and anger in people's faces, replacing them with a warm blanket of love spread across the person's soul. It's really kind of transformational when you see it.

We were in church one Sunday morning as our priest, Father Bob, was concluding Mass before the final blessing. He asked the congregation to open our hymnals to the back cover and recite with him the Prayer of St. Francis.

"Lord, make me an instrument of your peace. Where there is hatred, let me sow love. Where there is injury, pardon. Where there is doubt, faith. Where there is despair, hope. Where there is darkness, light. And where there is sadness, joy. O Divine Master, grant that I may not so much seek to be consoled as to console, to be understood as to understand, to be loved as to love." And this is what really hit me about this prayer. ***"For it is in giving that we receive.*** *It is in pardoning that we are pardoned.* ***And it is in the dying that we are born to eternal life."***

I can tell you straight up that as a full-time caregiver of a special-needs child, I do miss my "old life" sometimes. I miss the days when I'd pop on a new custom-made suit and shirt, jump on a airplane to some city in this country or another, and deliver an engaging keynote address or training session to a room full of accomplished go-getters and senior executives. However, that life seems as if it were a hundred years ago now. Maybe it's because I've gone through a bit of a transformation myself, thanks to Connor. In one sense, that former personality, that driven, hard-charging self, has died, and as a result, a new life in me has been born. It's just like the end of the prayer says. I truly believe this! A life less focused on me, and more focused on what I can do for others who are on this caregiver journey. This prayer has helped me see that things are indeed coming full circle around the principle of giving to give. Pretty amazing stuff!

Giving to give. Something I was taught as a young boy as the right way in which to approach people. I don't know where it all changed along the way, the notion of holding back until you know *exactly* with whom you're dealing. But it's a lesson that's been made real for me by my beautiful son, a boy with less cognitive ability than many, and perhaps more emotional depth and heartfelt capacity than most.

How much can we learn *and* gain from others when we focus first on giving to give, versus giving to get? Basic stuff, I know, and yet it took my cognitively challenged son to drive it home for me. What about you? It's something we can all practice more of—giving to give.

Personal Reflections Around Connor Principle Four
Give to Give

Reflect upon the following questions regarding how this principle shows up in your life as a caregiver. Write down your thoughts, and ask others involved in the caregiving to do the same. Then discuss them together, or with another caregiver who might be dealing with similar challenges. Here are the questions to consider and discuss:

1) How are you changing as a result of your special-needs child/children?
2) Have others noticed the changes?
3) What have you learned from your special-needs child/children that has caused a bit of a transformation in you, and/or in your family?

Having a morning chat with
his blanky, "Snuffy."

New toy saxophone
from Santa

APPROACH THE CLOSED

Who am I talking about? People like me, and other caregivers of special-needs children. Allow me to explain. When we got the news about Connor, I gradually shut down and closed myself off from the world over a number of years. The emotional trauma and mental exhaustion, which I had no experience in coping with, was hard for me to handle. I became closed off without even being aware of it. As a result, my family, friends, coworkers and clients didn't know *how* to approach me anymore. What to say? How to act? They were as confused about how to approach me, and my new situation, as I was hurting and closed off. Not a good thing.

Though I've mentioned it already, I find it amazing that various research and articles estimate there are approximately 35 million or more people in the United States alone who are parents or related caregivers to a special-needs child. So imagine **how many caregivers** might be in the process of shutting down or closing themselves off emotionally, psychologically or spiritually? It's got to be a significant number.

When caregivers shut down, it impacts **everyone**—the family, the parents' relationship, the special-needs children, the extended family, and all employer organizations. That's the scope of how it touches society, business, industry, the educational system, the medical establishment and the government—local, state and federal. The **financial ramifications** to all of us are something to take notice of because they are intense. And how will it affect us in the future, if caregivers don't get the emotional support, respite and ongoing encouragement they need?

Shutting down and closing off from the world was my situation for years, and I'm certainly not unique in this area. On any given day, there are probably thousands of caregivers of special-needs children who, at any one time, are in serious need of support from someone who has the emotional bandwidth to walk with them during very challenging, doubt-filled, and lonely times. And what an honorable way to help!

Caregiver or not, we can all learn to help each other (since the scope of this issue is enormous and ever-growing), by understanding the significant stresses and "bat-to-the-head" feeling that news of a child diagnosed with a special need transfers to the parents and extended family. By attempting to comprehend this level of shock, sadness and hopelessness, perhaps you will reach out and approach a caregiver **before** they close themselves off from the world, helping them, their family and their special-needs children. It's as critical as any humanitarian relief effort, **right here** in our own country. Look around! This issue is all around us.

Approach the closed. Oftentimes, those you approach won't understand they've closed themselves off from the world around them. They might want to be held while they cry, or they might want to be walked with, encouraged or listened to. And you can do this if you're someone who understands compassion. They're either coping with devastating news, and/or getting used to carrying a new cross for the rest of their lives. If you step in and help them carry it once in a while, you will help them find a new **resilience** within themselves to carry on and move forward as best they can. And maybe you'll get a few "brownie points" stored up for you in Heaven in the process.

Approach the closed. It *always* comes back to help you because it's the right thing to do!

PERSONAL REFLECTIONS AROUND CONNOR PRINCIPLE FIVE
APPROACH THE CLOSED

Reflect upon the following questions regarding how this principle shows up in your life as a caregiver. Write down your thoughts, and ask others involved in the caregiving to do the same. Then discuss them together, or with another caregiver who might be dealing with similar challenges. Here are the questions to consider and discuss:

1) Caregiver on not, make a plan to help another caregiver of a special-needs child, who may have closed themselves off from others without being aware of if. Figure out how to approach them and help them. Then **go do it** this week or next, and discuss what you learned from the experience.

2) Consider making the above practice part of your weekly routine. Giving to give is a pretty cool thing, especially when those you are giving to aren't expecting anything in return. Talk about a high!

Chilling in the lodge after
morning with ski instructor

First experience on the gondola.
He calls it the "gondagola"

OPEN YOUR MIND

Connor and I were all dressed up in downtown Minneapolis during the Christmas season, enjoying a holiday concert at Orchestra Hall featuring the fabulous and talented Doc Severinsen conducting the orchestra and choir. It's one of the traditions our family enjoys during the holidays.

I am always on edge during these beautiful concerts because, although Connor *lives* for music of all kinds, the sound of any saxophone or high-pitched trumpet can send him over the edge due to his massive sensitivity to certain loud and high-pitched sounds. As a safety precaution, I brought along his sound-deadening headphones, to prevent him from going into orbit if he heard any of these sounds, though it was hard to predict when they were coming.

Connor was having a wonderful time, proud to be a part of all the music, while watching his grandma Judy (my mom) sing in the choir. The first half went without interruption. But toward the end of the second half, while Connor was intently focused on the orchestra, Doc let his horn rip, hitting a high note for a prolonged period. I knew the song so I was prepared, clamping on his headphones in plenty of time. But it didn't do the trick this time. Connor heard the note, grabbed his ears over his headphones and starting kicking the backs of the seats in front of us, tears streaming down his cheeks. I picked him up, all 90 pounds, and quickly brought him out into the adjoining hallway, away from the loud trumpet sounds. I held him as he rocked back and forth, hands opening and closing in rapid succession, repeating how his ears hurt—and that he **wanted to go back in** and watch **more**! It is *unbelievably* challenging sometimes when these things occur, which is on a routine basis.

As people were leaving after the concert, we got the chance to go back stage and mingle with the orchestra, choir and Doc Severinsen. Standing in line as patiently as Connor knew how, holding my hand and attempting to wait, (something *very* difficult for him to do), asking repeatedly what we were waiting for, he took off. He broke through a crowd of people and security standing between us, and Doc, who I could see leaning in the doorway of a dressing room visiting with well-wishers. I took off after Connor, catching up with him just as he ran up to Doc, bear-hugging him, interrupting his conversation with other well-wishers, and said, *"You play too loud. Hurts my ears."* Can you imagine Johnny Carson saying that to Doc? Doc, being the gracious person he is, could see Connor rocking back and forth, and more than likely picked up that he might be a special-needs child. He engaged Connor in conversation, apologizing for playing his trumpet too loud as others looked on with astonishment that I would *allow* my child to speak to an accomplished musician in such a disrespectful manner! The looks I got from others close by were harsh. But Doc handled it all in perfect stride, not only by being kind and gentle with Connor, but also by engaging with him.

Appropriate exchange? For a special-needs child it can be typical, because you never know what they're going to say or do from time to time. What it did for me is **teach me** how "on edge" many of us are, including me, about what's appropriate and what's not, and that as a people, we've got **little tolerance** for *any* variation on what we view as *acceptable* behavior. We can often be harshly closed-minded about anything out of the ordinary, which this story was. Still, Doc seemed to find it delightfully refreshing—the honesty of it all.

This story, one of hundreds I could share, reminds me of how closed-minded I can be at times, which prevents me from the fuller experience I believe Connor is teaching me about life. I'm learning that it's okay, maybe even healthy, to open my mind to new experiences that perhaps aren't going to happen necessarily in the *appropriate* manner. And that it is okay to loosen up a bit, open my mind and enjoy the ride that Connor is taking me on.

If you allowed yourself to open your mind a bit more, what new experiences could you enjoy that might enrich your life and learning as a parent or related caregiver of a special-needs child?

PERSONAL REFLECTIONS AROUND CONNOR PRINCIPLE SIX
OPEN YOUR MIND

Reflect upon the following questions regarding how this principle shows up in your life as a caregiver. Write down your thoughts, and ask others involved in the caregiving to do the same. Then discuss them together, or with another caregiver who might be dealing with similar challenges. Here are the questions to consider and discuss:

1) What are some of the things your special-needs child does or doesn't do in public settings, that makes you either nervous, on edge, or full of anxiety? And how do you "get" when these things happen?
2) Is there anything to be learned when these things happen, or when you react the way that you do?
3) What would be something simple you could do or practice that would remind you to open your mind?

Relaxing by the fireplace

Hearing Angel Child performed
with full orchestra & choir

TRUST THE GUIDANCE

As a parent or related caregiver of a special-needs child, you are going to get **lots** of advice, suggestions, opinions and guidance from lots of people: doctors, lawyers, researchers, clinicians, licensed therapists, teachers, school administrators, paraprofessionals, counselors, mental health professionals, specialists, financial advisors, your parents, brothers, sisters, extended family members, your priest, minister, pastor, rabbi, therapist, and on and on and on. Some guidance will be welcomed and some not, as **everyone** seems to have an opinion on how to parent a special-needs child—even those who don't have one!

Be that as it may, only *you* will know for sure as you digest all the advice what guidance is right for you, your special-needs children and your family. So trust yourself, which is sometimes hard to do when you've been shaken up and down like salt and pepper shakers. Trust your instincts on the guidance that feels right to you.

You are going to go through periods where it may seem as though your whole life is being challenged; your outlook, your very nature, your career choices and your work, the goals and dreams that you have, and the manner in which you've been managing your life, etc. And I'm not kidding either. It might happen. In my case, it caused me to surrender, as I've shared earlier, to the notion that perhaps I was not the *ultimate* person in control, inviting more faith and guidance than ever before. This was and still is very hard for me to do, but it is like a daily walk of faith that everything is somehow going to work out. And I have trusted that guidance as a **roadmap** for the new life I am now trying to carve out of the experiences and life situations that have entered my life's path, with the hope that by offering them up and putting them out there, they will benefit many others on their own path.

Here is one example of how this principle of trusting the guidance has and continues to impact me. And why, if you are a woman, you may want your husband or significant other to read this as well. Pretty important stuff for the **men** to hear and digest.

As most of us would likely agree, it is often the woman who is typically considered the "caregiver" of the family—not the man. It is what it is. It's a pretty strong perception that this is the norm. Therefore, as a man, it is easy to feel frustrated in my role as a full-time caregiver, sometimes out of place, because of the lack of empathy and **respect** from other men who—when they learn I am the one who takes Connor to all of his doctor and therapist appointments, as well as his IEP meetings with special ed teachers, his main teachers, and paraprofessionals— I often catch this **attitude** from other men. It's often along the lines of, *"Don't you have **someone else** doing all of that? I mean, shouldn't you be **working**? Maybe you ought to find someone else, like maybe a nanny or something, that could do all of that, so you can work."* It is as if many men feel as though caregiving isn't their proper role or their bag, and that any man focused on that is somehow not doing his *job* as a man. Or, that caregiving is not *nearly* as important as their work, and that it ought to be *handled* by someone else.

Personally, this attitude is a crock! Caregiving of a special-needs child is as **hard** and **challenging** as anything I have *ever* done in business over the past 28 years—perhaps even more so. And it is hard work. Perhaps more men should experience that and they'd learn more about life, helping them become a more well-rounded and successful person as a result. Now there's a twist!

At the end of the day, when you are called to give an account for your life, you will not be measured nor judged by **how big your bank account was**, but rather, how your children turned out and are getting along in life, as well as how you treated others. This is just one example of where I practice Trusting the Guidance, because to me, what I am learning about being present in all of these things allows me to do a better job for Connor, so that he is the biggest beneficiary. And that's the way it ought to be in my humble opinion.

PERSONAL REFLECTIONS AROUND CONNOR PRINCIPLE SEVEN
TRUST THE GUIDANCE

Reflect upon the following questions regarding how this principle shows up in your life as a caregiver. Write down your thoughts, and ask others involved in the caregiving to do the same. Then discuss them together, or with another caregiver who might be dealing with similar challenges. Here are the questions to consider and discuss:

1) What guidance are you getting lately in regard to your special-needs child or children that doesn't ring true to you? Why?
2) What does your gut tell you to do in regard to this advice?
3) What would happen if you followed your gut?

Jazz festival on the mountain in Snowmass

Listening to music together
on the mountain

He loves to ski. He's so
very proud of himself!

CARVE YOUR FUTURE

Who ever thought that going to the local Target Greatland for routine grocery shopping would ever be so much fun? I certainly never did. But it's actually fun! This is an example of the new future we are carving together. Connor has become a literal "rock star" at our local Target store. He does this dance where, after we've filled up our shopping cart and are heading toward the checkout aisle, he begins chatting up his "girlfriends"—these wonderful cashiers who begin saying, "Hey, Connor. How's it going?" He then proceeds to give them all high-fives with the full fist-pump, as if he's just hit a grand slam in the World Series. He is **so proud** of himself as he carries on with all the ladies as we go through the checkout aisle, slyly trying to put candy into the cart that he feels we missed—without me seeing.

Before Connor's birth and the news of his diagnosis, my future (as I saw it) was pretty clear. It was just the way I liked it. Everything seemed to be in its rightful place and "on track"—the lingo for letting others and ourselves know we're in a good place and making progress. But when the diagnosis came, all of those plans and pictures went away overnight, and I lived for a period of *years* with no clear picture of what the future held for me, my family or my special-needs child. I was essentially in a trance. Not a good thing.

This can be a dangerous reality for any man, especially for those who are hard-charging, task-oriented, get-it-done, type-A people. I cannot speak to how women process information, stress and anxiety, when there are constant ups and downs and everything seems up in the air and totally fuzzy. I think it's safe to say, however, that nobody enjoys extended periods of confusion, anxiety and uncertainty about their future. But for caregivers of special-needs children, they must live from day to day with higher levels of uncertainty about the future. Sometimes this causes anxiety, depression or anger. Other times it can cause people to surrender a bit—opening up to receiving help from others, or from above, in those cases when you feel you have no one else to turn to for strength.

That being said, at some point, you will need to start carving your new future: new pictures, new dreams, new plans, a new or different work life that can better accommodate your responsibilities as a caregiver. You'll also need new family traditions around your life with a special-needs child. It won't all come together at once; so don't expect that it will. But after you process the initial trauma, the learning process begins. All the emotional adjustments begin to settle in your heart, and you start to regain some level of normalcy—if you dare call it that. And when this time comes for you, you'll intuitively know it's time for you to begin carving your new future, that you **can** do it, and that you **will** do it, because you have *way* too much to share that will help so many others along their path.

A highlight for Connor — performing in the marching band

Personal Reflections Around Connor Principle Eight
Carve Your Future

Reflect upon the following questions regarding how this principle shows up in your life as a caregiver. Write down your thoughts, and ask others involved in the caregiving to do the same. Then discuss them together, or with another caregiver who might be dealing with similar challenges. Here are the questions to consider and discuss:

1) Since the diagnosis of your special-needs child/children, what are a few things/activities you've begun doing together that you might consider new rituals or family traditions moving forward?

2) Do you enjoy doing them with your special-needs child/children?

3) List three things you would consider new family traditions you could all do together to bring newfound laughter and happiness into your life. Then, start doing them, and begin carving your new future together.

4) What do you need to do to **protect** your own **sanity** in your new life as a caregiver? Make the commitment to yourself to do these things. This is very important on your path to carving a new future that works for everyone: you, your spouse/significant other, your family and your special-needs children.

First year skiing together
Snowmass Colorado

Photo opp on the mountain

SHARE YOUR EXPERIENCE

As children, we're taught to share. We're told that it's not only important, but what life is really all about. But sadly, as we grow into adulthood, this early teaching seems to get pushed to the wayside of life.

As parents and related caregivers of special-needs children, I believe we've been given the special *calling* of sharing our challenges, stories, doubts, fears and special moments with other caregivers that could benefit from learning about our lives—our challenges, and what we've learned as a result. I'm not suggesting you become a full-time motivational speaker. But more than likely, there are things you've learned along your path that could and would help others on theirs.

Some people believe that intense hardships, challenges or extreme difficulties actually sculpt the heart, soul and character of a person into a more complete picture of who they're designed to be. If you are one who believes in this line of thinking, then trust that **your** experience, whatever that is, is indeed worth sharing with other caregivers. Your lessons learned could be of genuine benefit to them. Consider sharing your experience. Isn't *that* what life is all about?

One simple **caution** from one caregiver to another as people ask you what it's like to parent a special-needs child. Ask them if they are a caregiver first. There's usually a reason they're asking you questions. Second, if we've had a difficult week or two, I have at times **unloaded** way too much about what it's really like—the ups and downs—to people who've not been caregivers, and they'll look at me as though I'm embellishing, which ends up bumming me out for the rest of the day. Remember, non-caregivers may have high regard for all they see you do, either at church, at the grocery store, etc., and want to encourage you by asking you what it's like. Therefore, be gentle with them. Perhaps you don't need to unload, as they won't know how to process it all. It's nice they are asking, so remember that. However, if another **caregiver** is asking you to share, rest assured, it is probably a bit safer to share the good, the bad and the ugly, since there is an unspoken respect and camaraderie among caregivers of special-needs children, and a genuine desire to help lift one another up. We're all in the same club!

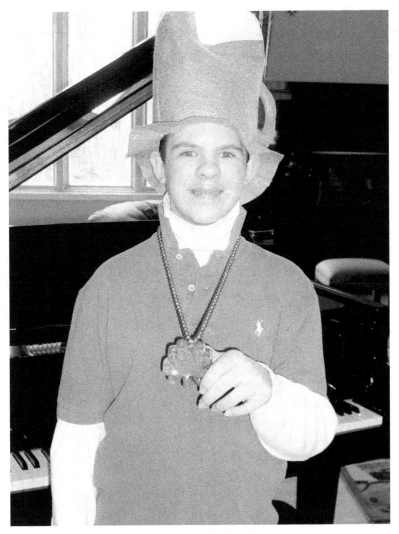

Celebrating St. Patrick's Day

Personal Reflections Around Connor Principle Nine
Share Your Experience

Reflect upon the following questions regarding how this principle shows up in your life as a caregiver. Write down your thoughts, and ask others involved in the caregiving to do the same. Then discuss them together, or with another caregiver who might be dealing with similar challenges. Here are the questions to consider and discuss:

1) What are two or three things you are most proud of as a parent or related caregiver of a special-needs child/children?

2) What would you say are the two or three things that have been the biggest lessons learned for you?

3) How have you and your family changed as a result of parenting/raising a special-needs child?

4) What would be your advice or suggestions (two or three things) to parents who have recently learned their child/children have been diagnosed with a special need or two?

Telling me about his day
on the mountain

His second part in Mary
Poppins--a chimney sweep

Embrace Your Child

Everyone gets surprises thrown at them during their lifetime. It is simply unavoidable. Some are small and relatively easy to deal with. Others are more significant, often causing pain, anxiety, stress and maybe even a setback or two. But over a relatively short period of time, you learn to deal with the surprise or disappointment, and move through the experience, hopefully to a better place.

When you're the parent of a special-needs child, however, it's a PERMANENT surprise! One that raises the bar on all sorts of emotions, some you never knew you even had. It can totally eclipse you. I've seen it happen with caregivers, including me. It can be such a *permanent life jolt* that some can't recover—can't get back on the horse of life. This can become a serious issue for the caregiver, their family and the special-needs children, if not resolved or dealt with in some manner.

In these situations, a huge level of resentment can come out toward the special-needs child or children, family or spouse/significant other—none of whom deserve it because it's not anyone's fault. Therefore, instead of fostering resentment toward your special-needs child because your world may now be turned upside down, I have learned to slow way down. **Cut back on or cut out** any and all activities that add to the anxiety and stress of life with your special-needs child. This helps you embrace them, and learn from them. I'm not trying to sound all rosy and Pollyannish. Instead, this is what I've had to do to protect my own mental health, outlook and well-being, so I speak from firsthand experience, versus some out-there philosophy.

If that sounds too rosy, then perhaps getting some professional help might be a good solution. It can help you learn to calm down, get rid of the toxic resentments toward life or whomever, and prepare you to experience the true power of what special-needs children can teach us all, though you might not yet be at a place where you are open to being "taught" anything from your special-needs child or children.

However, **hear me** right now! **Do not push them away** because you're resentful that your life might now be anxiety-ridden, overly stressful, complex and hard. It's **not** always going to be that way, and **it's not their fault!** Get help with these legitimate feelings so you can experience and embrace your special-needs child. One final story that might help bring this last Connor Principle home.

It was the fall of 2010, a busy school-day morning and for whatever reason, I was irritated and anxious about not getting enough done regarding my work due to all the various things I needed to do for Connor. It felt like I was falling behind, and, of course, for us taskmaster-type folks, falling behind bothers us. I'd dropped Connor off at school around 9:10 a.m. and headed back to my office to get some writing done and phone calls made. However, no sooner did I get rolling on my work than his school called saying he was in the office lying down complaining of stomach pains, and that he wanted me to come get him. So, I dropped everything, whipped up to school, brought him home, checked his temperature (which was okay) and put him down in his own bed to rest. About an hour later, he was still holding his stomach and weeping.

In to Southdale Pediatrics we went to see the doctor, who astutely felt it was likely his appendix after poking around his tummy. Being a Friday afternoon with no CT scanning gear in their offices, she booked us into the emergency room at Children's Hospital in downtown Minneapolis. Back in the Jeep we went, flew down to Children's where they were waiting for us. We signed in and immediately went into prep for the CT scan of his stomach to see what was going on. Sure enough, they felt his appendix had *already* ruptured from what they could tell from the scan. Without a moments notice, I was standing in front of the anesthesiologist as he explained how they were going to put him down due to his Williams Syndrome and his related heart issues, with his aortic stenosis. After I authorized that, the surgeon stepped forward, introduced himself, shared what the scan showed him and how he felt we should proceed. Talk about professionals! These people were top-notch and kind. And Connor was a champ, as he gets **very** anxious about getting a "pinch," his language for getting a shot—or two or three, as it was in this case, since they had to put him under.

As I walked beside his hospital bed into the operating room, he was clenching my hand tightly, even though he was half on his way to slumber. Once in the operating room, they gently slid the mask over his face with the bubble-gum scent he had picked out as they introduced the anesthesia into his system, and wham, he was out. Something that *always* shakes me up. They showed me to the waiting room saying the surgery should take between 90-120 minutes, and they'd call me around 1 a.m. or so when he was in recovery. There I sat with my mom and a good friend, worrying about whether his appendix had already ruptured, and all that might be ahead.

It was a long wait. The phone rang and the nurse said it went well, that they got it right before it was about to rupture, that he was in recovery sleeping, and that I could go see him in about an hour. Though it was good news, I was still worried. Just my nature I guess. As I entered the recovery room, there he was, already holding court with both the nurses assigned to him as he quickly learned he could have whatever flavor popsicles he wanted—one after the other, within reason of course, which means nothing to Connor, other than, "I can have a hundred or so if I want!"

As he was chatting up the nurses, working them for another popsicle or two, he'd look at them, reach out his hand for theirs, clasp it, and then say ever so genuinely; *"I need you in my life. I just need you in my life,"* charming them as best he could in order to get another popsicle. Pretty clever indeed, until I had to say we'd had enough due to his sugar issues. What a charmer! "I need you in my life." Wow. Maybe I should try that line sometime?

As he continued to fixate on the IV's still in his arms, trying to take them out, causing the nurse to tape them down good and tight, he leaned over to me and said, *"Dad, are you having a hard day? I think you're having a hard day. I know it's hard, but we'll make it through."* That—made me cry. My boy was sensing how worried I was and telling me that **it was all going to be okay!**

You and I are going to encounter various things throughout our lives as care-givers of special-needs children that will be well beyond our control, requiring lots of patience, lots of faith, and lots of emotional bandwidth to trust that we'll make it through, regardless of what comes.

It is this uncertainty, if you will, that might actually help us to embrace our special-needs children, as it seems that sometimes they can sense what we need faster than we can. And in the beauty of the embrace, we are reminded of the very special journey we've been called to on behalf our special-needs children. **Embrace Your Child** and feel what comes as a result.

Lunch on the mountain

PERSONAL REFLECTIONS AROUND CONNOR PRINCIPLE TEN
EMBRACE YOUR CHILD

Reflect upon the following questions regarding how this principle shows up in your life as a caregiver. Write down your thoughts, and ask others involved in the caregiving to do the same. Then discuss them together, or with another caregiver who might be dealing with similar challenges. Here are the questions to consider and discuss:

1) Can you honestly say that regardless of the issues surrounding your special-needs child/children, you have embraced them with all of your heart, though the future ahead might well be full of challenges and unknowns?

2) What are you most concerned or worried about moving forward?

3) What is the best way to deal with these concerns in your opinion?

4) What is the one thing that would help you further embrace your special-needs child or the special-needs child/children you are caring for?

CAREGIVERS SPEAK—SUMMARY DISCUSSION QUESTIONS

In addition to the questions at the end of each Connor Principle Personal Reflection Section, you can also use the following questions in your small group discussions with family members and other caregivers of special-needs children within your Church congregation, at your favorite coffee shop, or anywhere that's comfortable. They can serve to help remind us all that, by sharing our own story, experiences, challenges, frustrations, fears, doubts, lessons and special moments, we can indeed help support one another along our own paths as caregivers—an important mission for each and every one of us. Here are the questions to consider and discuss:

1) How has your own faith changed since becoming a parent or related caregiver of a special-needs child?

2) How are you different as a person since the diagnosis of your special-needs child/children?

3) Looking back, how has having a special-needs child changed or impacted the entire family, even your extended family? And how has it impacted your marriage or relationship with your life partner?

4) What are the concerns or issues within you or your family that have been difficult to discuss or address, that need to be addressed or dealt with for the betterment of everyone involved in the caregiving journey?

5) Do you believe that God has chosen you to parent and raise a special-needs child? And what are you learning as a result? Are these lessons you could help other caregivers with?

6) Are you a better person as a result of parenting/raising a special-needs child? How or why do you think you are a better person because of the experience?

7) Share a special or touching moment you've had with your special-needs child and how it changed you, or made you feel as though you were called to parent this child or children?

8) Share some things that used to be **very** important to you, that now, since raising a special-needs child, don't seem as important as they once were. What have you learned from this change in priorities?

9) Of the 10 Connor Principles, which ones do you struggle with the most? Would it make sense to arrange a weekly coffee, phone call or email "check in" with another caregiver on the specific Connor Principles you are struggling with? If so, make a plan to do so, helping move you forward.

10) Regarding your caregiver journey, what you are most grateful for, and why?

COMING FULL CIRCLE—PRACTICE BRINGS PROGRESS

In review, The Connor Principles are timeless, genuine, forthright principles designed to be used and applied in your everyday journey as a caregiver of a special-needs child. They can help you reduce stress, anxiety, fear, doubt and worry, and replace the intensity of these emotions with a newfound energy and sense of purpose, helping empower you and your family on the journey ahead. If you embrace these principles in your everyday life, chances are that as you work on them, answering the Personal Reflection Questions at the end of each Connor Principle and doing the suggested exercises, you will likely put yourself, your family and your special-needs child/children in a better place to experience a deeper peace and calm along your path—perhaps even a renewed energy and feeling of being more empowered. This is why I am asking you to bring them full circle, so they *can* have a positive impact in your life, and your family's life.

There is a reason you and I have been blessed with a special-needs child. Sometimes, it would sure be nice to have a little insight from above as to why these children have been given to us. But in the absence of this insight, this is where faith plays a role in each of our lives, giving us the opportunity to either grow in faith, hope, courage and belief—or not. It's as simple as that. We all get to choose, since we've all been given free will. My sincere hope is that you will use, apply and take to heart the true power that lies within The Connor Principles by making them a part of your own life moving forward.

If you feel that this book has helped you, please visit The Reach For Me Network website and share your feedback. And if you feel it has been beneficial, please share it with other members of your family involved in the caregiving, as well as friends, co-workers and members of your church who are caregivers as well.

Thank you. Be blessed, move forward and Embrace Your Child!
—Michael A. Boylan

ABOUT THE REACH FOR ME NETWORK

Caring For The Caregiver™

Emotional Support, Recognition, Empowerment

Financial Savings on Products & Services For Caregivers

Advocacy

The Reach For Me Network is addressing one of the most compelling issues of our time facing millions of parents and related caregivers of special-needs children of any diagnosis—cognitive or physical—and all employer organizations, as it is estimated that 10 percent or more of a company's employees are caregivers of special-needs children.

Based on various research and articles, it has been reported that as many as **one** in **five** families in the U.S. (20 percent) have or are caring for a special-needs child or children. This translates to upwards of 35 million parents and related caregivers in the U.S. alone impacted emotionally, spiritually, psychologically and financially. It also impacts employer organizations financially in areas such as the volume of medical claims, insurance premiums, morale and employee productivity, absenteeism, turnover, creativity, ability to focus, and level of enthusiasm on the job. Hence, the issue directly impacts the financial health and productivity of all companies. And because the federal and state governments are **reducing** the budgets for special-needs children of any diagnosis, which parents so desperately need and depend on for various services, the **only** way to respond to this truth is to **band together** and **help one another** by becoming a very powerful **force** nationwide, similar in some respects to how senior citizens have banded together through AARP. Reach For Me could be considered the "AARP/Facebook/Groupon" for parents and related caregivers of special-needs children nationwide, and eventually, internationally.

The Reach For Me Network is addressing this broad-reaching issue through an online community of caregivers of special-needs children sharing their stories and challenges, their knowledge and experience, inspiration, emotional support and encouragement with other like-minded caregivers, providing a web of support, trust, recognition, empathy and ongoing encouragement for millions of caregivers. The Reach For Me Network is a safe haven where those with much in common can help one another throughout the caregiver journey, since no one understands or empathizes with this life more than other caregivers.

The network also endeavors to help caregivers save hundreds, if not **thousands** of dollars **every year** through a special buying club by aggregating parents and related caregivers of special-needs children who represent a **sizeable** population needing more of certain kinds of products and services, such as life insurance, long-term care and disability insurance, medical insurance, trust and estate planning, financial planning services, legal services, medications, and numerous other products and services. By banding together, we create the leverage necessary with large corporations that wish to sell us their products and services, helping members save money on the kinds of products and services caregivers need. It will give caregivers the **leverage, power** and **recognition** they deserve to negotiate with corporations who wish to recognize caregivers through more favorable pricing on their products and services for members of the RFM Network.

Over time, plans are to also offer caregivers a physical network in local communities throughout the country, where they can attend support group meetings with other parents of special-needs children through their church congregations. Certified Facilitators—licensed, certified and trained by Reach For Me, will host these meetings focused on supporting and empowering caregivers.

To provide a network of ongoing emotional and psychological support, encouragement, information, inspiration, recognition and friendship for like-minded people who share a common bond—parents and related caregivers of special-needs children. The network will provide a place for members to share hope, understanding and knowledge through the online community, outreach meetings, and through employer organizations via enterprise memberships in the network for their own employee caregivers.

The purpose is to **reduce stress** and **anxiety** on employee caregivers and their families; reduce caregiver absenteeism, turnover and burnout; decrease medical claims of all kinds, insurance premiums and related costs to organizations; and increase caregiver productivity, focus, attitude and commitment to the enterprise. Reach For Me is about **taking better care of the caregiver**, so they can take better care of their special-needs children and families and be more productive for the organizations that employ them.

There is currently no "one-stop shop" such as Reach For Me focused on parents and related caregivers of special-needs children. Although there are individual support groups, there is no **national umbrella organization** focused on the emotional, inspirational and informational needs of caregivers, regardless of the diagnosis of the child—cognitive or physical.

Most services focus primarily around the children's diagnosis, such as raising money to fund research to find a cure for a particular diagnosis. Reach For Me (RFM) is for and about the caregivers: **Caring for the caregivers of special-needs children** of any diagnosis. This is the key differentiator. As stated, the goal of the site is threefold:

1. Helping caregivers find continued **emotional support, inspiration** and **motivation** to keep moving forward.

2. **Leveraged Purchasing Power/Buying Club.** Aggregating parents and related caregivers of special-needs children into one place, thereby providing substantial financial savings on numerous products and services we all routinely need. Making caregivers' lives easier and less stressful by helping them save money on the daily necessities of life, such as food, clothing, medications, life, long-term care and medical insurance, household items, financial planning services, legal services, etc., by giving them leveraged purchasing power. Over time, the site intends to provide information on issues related to improving the quality of life for caregivers.

3. **Nationwide Advocacy.** The marketplace understands, respects and responds to other organizations possessing the same thing: **power, momentum** and **leverage** to *drive* change. By millions of parents of special-needs children of **all** diagnoses banding together, the network becomes a **force** for positive change on behalf of all members, causing positive change in what we pay for things, such as health insurance, prescription drugs, life insurance, financial planning services, legal services, extra levels of education and care for our children, etc. The network intends to provide advocacy for our members as we band together creating the leverage, influence and power necessary to facilitate positive benefits for all.

Fortune 2000 and mid-sized organizations can purchase an **Enterprise Membership** in the network under their health and wellness oriented benefits, allowing employee-caregivers within the organization to join the network at no charge. This allows employee-caregivers to participate, as they desire, in the online community, support group meetings, Caregiver Weekend Summits, and other ongoing training/coaching-oriented programs. This provides employee-caregivers (10+ percent of the employee population) the support and inspiration they need on an ongoing basis.

The financial benefit to the organization is enhanced employee loyalty, productivity and commitment to the enterprise, and a reduction in absenteeism, turnover, insurance claims, premiums and litigation, which cost organizations dearly. For a list of products, services, programs and enterprise membership options for organizations of all sizes, please visit our website:

www.ReachForMeNetwork.com

Join the Groundswell
Enterprise Memberships
Become a Certified Facilitator

If you are an executive with an employer, please contact us to discuss **enterprise membership options** in The Reach For Me Network. Your membership will allow employee-caregivers within your company to join at no charge. They'll receive the emotional support, encouragement, recognition and inspiration they need to keep moving forward at home, and at work.

If you are a **caregiver**, join The Reach For Me Network and start receiving the emotional support and ongoing encouragement you deserve to help you keep moving forward in challenging times.

If you are a caregiver interested in becoming a **Certified Facilitator** so that you can **share your own caregiver journey** with hundreds of other caregivers through the facilitation of **Caregiver Weekend Summits** in your area, please visit our website and schedule a **conference call** with an RFM staff member to learn more about this exciting way to help support and empower other caregivers in your area.

INVITE THE AUTHOR TO SPEAK
AT YOUR ORGANIZATION OR CHURCH

The founder of The Reach For Me Network, Michael A. Boylan, is one of the highest rated, most engaging and qualified keynote speakers in the country, having addressed groups from a few hundred to 7,500 attendees for 15+ years. He consistently receives high marks from all organizations because of his genuine and interactive style, his ability to draw out and engage all attendees, regardless of the size of the group he is addressing, and the lasting value that everyone feels they have received.

Michael can tailor his address to meet and achieve the objectives of your event, meeting or conference. To learn more regarding rates and availability, please contact The Reach For Me Network to share the date of your meeting or conference, goals for the event, number of attendees, etc.

CAREGIVER WEEKEND SUMMIT
CONNOR PRINCIPLES FAMILY HOME STUDY PROGRAM

When was the last time you had a genuine break? You probably can't remember. The Caregiver Weekend Summit is a **life-changing** and empowering three-day program for married and single caregivers and their families, sharing a process that can help reduce stress and anxiety within the family, while promoting perspective, greater understanding, clarity, and more peace.

And in the event you are unable to attend a Caregiver Weekend Summit somewhere in the country, The Connor Principles Family Home Study Program is designed for **self-facilitation** by the primary caregiver(s) to help the entire family reduce stress and anxiety and promote perspective, greater understanding, clarity and family unity. Please visit the website for additional information on both programs. They are designed to help!

Angel Child Anthem Song—Angel Child Music Video

With a lyric designed to honor, recognize and pay tribute to "a-day-in-the-life" of caregivers of special-needs children and the music video designed to do the same, "Angel Child" can inform and educate society at large on the scope of this issue. If you have yet to get a copy of the song and music video, please visit **www.ReachForMeNetwork.com** to purchase your piece of recognition to share with others in your life, helping them understand the journey you are on.

Written by the founder during a particular low point, the music and lyric share a conversation between the parents pushing back at life with all of their questions about, *"Why did you give me this special-needs child?"* and the special-needs children responding back to their parents in the chorus of the song, saying, *"Reach For Me, I'll show you the way. Reach For Me, I'll lighten your day."*

Designed to bring attention to the challenges and the joys of parenting a special-needs child/children, "Angel Child" has been called the *"We Are The World"* of our time. Get your copy of the song and music video and join the network today!

Follow-Up Books Coming in Time

Watch for more books coming down the road, as there are three more planned at this time. Each one goes deeper into the core content of *The Connor Principles* and the power of their useful applications in your life and at work. They'll also be helpful for your other children, who sometimes need help comprehending and gaining perspective on what it's like to have a brother or sister who is a special-needs child.

Share Your Thoughts On This Book

We welcome your thoughts, comments and feedback on *Reach For Me, The Story of My Son Connor*: what you have gained from the book, how it has served to inspire you in some form or fashion, and how you plan to apply *The Connor Principles* in your own life as a caregiver of a special-needs child. Please email us with your feedback at info@ReachForMeNetwork.com

Endorsement From Personal Experience

You may have noticed the picture on the back cover—Connor and I walking toward the location of this summer music and dance camp for special-needs children of any diagnosis—cognitive or physical, which I have taken Connor to for the last seven summers. This camp, in addition to the ski programs in which I have enrolled him, is helping his overall cognitive, fine and gross motor skills development. He loves the programs and always looks forward to going. I speak as a father of a special-needs child **and** customer of the program. I know the founder and some of the management. They are committed people, focused on giving your child a wonderful, memory-rich, safe and fun experience.

It's called "Challenge Aspen," a year-round, nonprofit offering recreational, cultural, competitive and educational opportunities for children with cognitive and physical challenges and disabilities. To learn more, check out the website at www.ChallengeAspen.com.

THE MAKING OF ANTHEM SONG AND MUSIC VIDEO
ANGEL CHILD

On April 6, 2013, on the campus of St. Olaf College in Northfield, Minnesota (after recording the rhythm session and click track at East West Recording Studios in Los Angeles), we recorded *Angel Child* with the 90-piece St. Olaf Orchestra and 75-voice choir; involving 600-plus parents and their special-needs children in this moving experience. Parents and their children had the opportunity to be involved in the creation of this emotional and meaningful recording!

I wish to thank the St. Olaf College Orchestra and Choir for their heartfelt commitment and passion to this project, and also acknowledge their outstanding musicianship and maturity for wanting to be involved in an outreach effort of this magnitude called The Reach For Me Network.

The song was mixed and mastered back in Los Angeles, with the editing of the music video taking place in Minneapolis. Below is a collection of photographs sharing a portion of the behind-the-scenes of *The Making of Angel Child.*

The song, music video and the behind-the-scenes *Making of Angel Child* 70-minute documentary are available for purchase on the website at www.ReachForMeNetwork.com, or on iTunes.

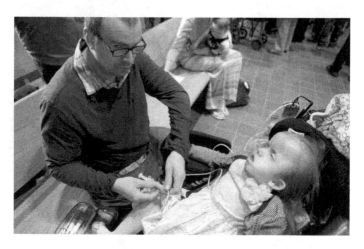

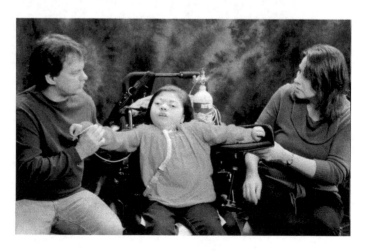

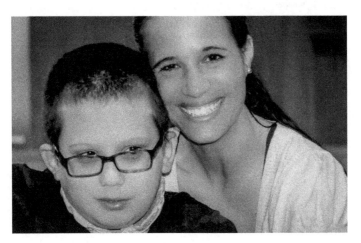

CARING FOR THE CAREGIVERS OF SPECIAL-NEEDS CHILDREN
REGARDLESS OF THE DIAGNOSIS OF THE CHILD

PLEASE CONTACT US

The Reach For Me Network

Carlson Center, 601 Carlson Parkway, Suite 1050

Minnetonka, Minnesota, 55305

Office: 952–449–5115

Web Site: www.ReachForMeNetwork.com

Printed in the USA
CPSIA information can be obtained
at www.ICGtesting.com
JSHW012050140824
68134JS00035B/3358

9 781683 500230